Black Bone

Senior Editor and Publisher: Frank X Walker
Project Editors: Bianca Lynne Spriggs & Jeremy Paden
Design and Layout: Carly Schnur

Black Bone is published by:

pluck! The Journal of Affrilachian Arts & Culture
University of Kentucky
1215 Patterson Office Tower
Lexington, KY 40506-0027

Reprinted by The University Press of Kentucky, 2018

ISBN 978-0-8131-7523-2 (pbk. : alk. paper)
ISBN 978-0-8131-7524-9 (pdf)
ISBN 978-0-8131-7525-6 (epub)

25 YEARS OF THE
AFFRILACHIAN POETS

Black
Bone

EDITED BY BIANCA LYNNE SPRIGGS & JEREMY PADEN

In memory of Rane Arroyo and Norman Jordan—rest in power.

Root

Limb

Tongue

SHAUNA M. MORGAN

Preface

25 Years of Revolutionary Art: Cultural Cartography and the Expanding Landscape of Affrilachian Poetics

"Any portrait of land worth its salt must also include a landscape of its people worth its weight in blood, sweat, and tears" opens Nikky Finney's review of *Affrilachia*, Frank X Walker's first book of poems (213). Indeed, Walker's debut collection named and helped to define a region and its people. Appearing in the *Journal of Appalachian Studies* alongside Chad Berry's essay "Upon What Will I Hang My Hat in the Future? Appalachia and Awaiting Postmodernity," Finney's review marked a propitious entry into the critical terrain of Appalachian Studies. Berry's piece, which asks important, existential questions such as "What is Appalachia?" does so with little consideration for a non-white Appalachia. Rather, it laments the postmodern thrust which attends to representation, and argues that "it is time to begin examining what Appalachia is and move beyond what it is not" (Berry 126). Finney's review ironically notes what Berry fails to fully consider: Appalachia is, in fact, a map of racial and ethno-cultural heterogeneity. She declares that Walker's *Affrilachia* "… carves out a twenty-first-century almanac of human geography that illuminates where the waterways of human hearts and blades of bluegrass meet to form a new/old sacred ground. It is an essential collection of poetry that must be included in the rich literary tradition of Appalachia, else half the story be told" (Finney 215).

Certainly, the corpora of Frank X Walker's and Nikky Finney's work formed the bedrock of what stands as Affrilachian Cultural Cartography. As the progenitors who collectively make up the fountainhead of the Affrilachian Poets, Walker and Finney exemplified the map-making and fostered the kinship of which bell hooks speaks in her text *Belonging: A Place of Culture*. The space of their community made "connections between geographical location and psychological states of being" and remained committed to "strategies of resistance that were life enhancing" and rooted in strong family values and an unbreakable connection to the ancestor (19). Walker's designation, Affrilachia, clearly emerged from a keen understanding of the multiple rootedness of the folks he located in that reality. The founding members of the Affrilachian Poets were all engaged in mapping Blackness both as race and culture, but even more importantly as an idea or consciousness emerging in and shaped by the region and its connection to a global awareness of liberation. These artists, who number almost forty today, continue to shape the literary landscape within and beyond the region. Frank X Walker's effort to "[challenge] the notion of a homogeneous all-white literary landscape" in Appalachia can be described as a form of what Evie Shockley describes as "Renegade Poetics" when moments of "race-related wrangling has led the poet beyond what experience has shown will do the job and into a space of formal risk-taking" (Shockley 9). Walker's innovation does not stand alone, however, as the entire collective has taken on the malevolence of a region and nation still mired in its legacy of heinous misdeeds, and has crafted linguistically daring poetry which journeys from the page into lived experiences and back again. In some instances, as with the work of Ricardo Nazario y Colón, the text marks an internal poetic revolution (*a veces sólo en Español*) that is deeply intimate and restraining in content and form.

The Affrilachian Poets have spent two and half decades not only producing work with a distinctive poetics of liberation, they also continue to mount a formidable movement against the myth of an all-white region while also documenting those nuanced realities of an ever-changing U.S. American South. Critic Kathryn Trauth Taylor argues that Affrilachian writing works as "performative rhetorical ecologies as a way of recognizing, conceiving, and valuing groups who live within the liminal, or "in-between" spaces of culture" (par 3). I contend, however, that this is not an interposal peculiarity; Affrilachia is, in fact, central to the Appalachian experience. To speak of the emergence of Appalachia without Africans and African-descended people would not only be naïve, but also inaccurate; this has been true in every aspect of production—cultural, social, economic, and otherwise. Especially among the Affrilachian Poets there exists a broad cultural reach which extends beyond genre and discipline. Theirs is an aesthetic of liberation that should never be mistaken for a kind of singular protest literature with "an appeal to white morality" (Neal 185). Rather, we must acknowledge the Affrilachian Poets' liberatory practice of producing work for an audience of people about whom they write. Like the community formed by Wallace Thurman, Langston Hughes, Zora Neale Hurston, Aaron Douglas and others who came together to launch *Fire!! A Quarterly Devoted to the Younger Negro Artists*, or the mid-twentieth century Black Arts Movement writers, who, in their quest to rediscover "the revolutionary potential in Blackness itself," the Affrilachian Poets' purposeful work stands in a tradition of the most dynamic and impactful writing of our time (Henderson 183). One need only look at Walker's historical poetry or his most recent collection, *Affrilachian Sonnets*, which at once covers the vast cultural and natural landscape, even as it deals with intimate familial relationships. The tradition of storytelling, linked to the lineages of Zora Neale Hurston and Alice Walker, flower in the fiction of Crystal Wilkinson. The timbre and rhythms of Appalachia resound in her short stories and new novel *The Birds of Opulence*, and the worlds of her narratives present an undeniable Affrilachia which lives in the soil, the rivers, the trees—even in the very air we breathe. Just as with its emergence, the future of Appalachia is inextricable from Affrilachia and its cultural producers. Bianca Lynne Spriggs' brilliance in visual art, poetry, and film (and, quite frankly, in any medium she sees fit), pushes the boundaries of our imaginations deep into realms still unknown.

The fans and followers of Affrilachian Poets, much like the faces who comprise the worlds of their texts, are scattered throughout the region and globally, and they bear witness to an art that is coupled with abounding activist work buttressed by bold political stances. Even though many APs have found homes in the academy, they persist in their resistance to it and other neoliberal forces, and move to create dissent in the face of evolving injustice. In their quarter of a century, the Affrilachian Poets' art, life, and activist work, have marked the region and the country in indelible and extraordinary ways. What of this art, then— these words—as Jeremy Paden has written—which are "sweet to the tongue / but bitter to the belly" of many (lines 8–9)? This art thrives. It grows. It moves beyond the region, out into our troubled nation, and even beyond the continent to forge a new world, to stand up for justice, and to call truth's name in ink and song.

Works Cited

Berry, Chad. "Upon What Will I Hang My Hat in the Future? Appalachia and Awaiting Post-Postmodernity." *Journal of Appalachian Studies*. 6 (2000): 121–130. Print.

Finney, Nikky. "Book Review: Affrilachia." *Journal of Appalachian Studies*. 6 (2000): 213–215. Print.

Henderson, Stephen E. *Understanding the New Black Poetry: Black Speech and Black Music As Poetic References*. New York: Morrow, 1973. Print.

hooks, bell. *Belonging: A Culture of Place*. New York: Routledge, 2009. Print.

Neal, Larry. "The Black Arts Movement." *Within the Circle: An Anthology of African American Literary Criticism from the Harlem Renaissance to the Present*. Angelyn Mitchell, Ed.

Durham: Duke University Press, 1994. Print.

Paden, Jeremy. "Honey and Wormwood." *Broken Tulips: Poems*. Lexington, KY: Accents Publishing, 2013. p. 10. Print.

Shockley, Evie. *Renegade Poetics: Black Aesthetics and Formal Innovation in African American Poetry*. Iowa City: University of Iowa Press, 2011. Print.

Taylor, Kathryn Trauth. "Naming Affrilachia: Toward Rhetorical Ecologies of Identity Performance in Appalachia." *Enculturation*: *A Journal of Rhetoric, Writing, and Culture*. 21 June 2011. Web.

Introduction

Affrilachia is both a geographic and a cultural space. And, as Shauna M. Morgan in her preface and Paul C. Taylor in the opening essay of this anthology note, it is also an ongoing literary and political concept shaped by the intent to lend voice to the voiceless.

There is a temptation when thinking in regionalist, aesthetic, and even political terms to go narrow, to say that this but not that may be admitted into the canon. Literary scholars are quite in love with drawing boundaries, as erecting finite borders fuels our modes of thinking. It is in our nature to classify and qualify genre to establish order and make sense of the abstract, but also to exert a kind of control. And, while it is true that the Affrilachian Poets, founded by a small group of students and professors, were born at the University of Kentucky, early on, they recognized the expansive nature of this new venture. They could imagine a prehistoric world where perhaps, before the drifting away of tectonic plates, the Appalachian Region and the West Coast of Africa were once merged. Thus, the term Affrilachia as both theory and practice might be viewed as a way of reuniting two disparate sides of one family tree.

It is in the spirit of creating inclusive cultural and spiritual spaces that the founding members of the Affrilachian Poets opened up the term to include all thirteen states touched by the mountain chain that gives us our name, whether in the south or the north. Furthermore, they opened up the term to include all portions of those states, whether in the coastal plains, riparian zones, plateaus and foothills, or the mountains proper, as a way to continue the conversation that region may operate as a cultural space and blur borders. While this widening of the lens corresponds directly to the political project of Affrilachia, this does not mean the collective ignores the importance of place as a wellspring for community and the imagination, to cite some positive benefits of regionalism. Or, how regions get bound to national myths and stereotypes, to cite some of the possible negative pressures that being from a place might give.

Along with deciding to open up the term Affrilachian to include poets from Louisville, Danville and Conway, South Carolina, the collective also decided that aesthetic freedom was preferable to a group centered around formal restrictions. The early leaders decided that along with experiments in shaping language, there should be a commitment to telling the overlooked stories of this place called Affrilachia.

Likewise, and as the name unequivocally signals, Affrilachia is rooted in the African diaspora and is largely a collective of writers whose roots trace back to the forced migrations of the Atlantic Slave Trade. Yet, and this is part of the inclusive nature of this collective, over the years, the group has brought in writers of Hispanic, Arab, Filipino, Hindu, and Chinese descent. At times, the geographical, aesthetic, and racial diversity of the group, have caused critics to wonder whether the Affrilachian Poets are a true collective of writers working toward a recognizable goal. But, the fuzzy geographical boundaries, the importance placed on story and witness over stylistic homogenity, and the occasional welcoming in of writers whose history of migration to these mountains is different than the majority of group, are not from an intellectual or aesthetic sloppiness, but from the political and ethical call at the heart of the group to name and tell the stories not attended to when Appalachia is understood only as white.

The impulse to be geographically inclusive allows our spectrum of members to identify with the challenges and mysteries of the region no matter where we are in the world. No matter where we hail from originally or where we move towards next, to be Affrilachian is to carry the pulse of the mountains within us. We are their allies. We are their kin. Affrilachia's expansiveness comes from paying attention to the margins and noting how, like with the top and bottom edges of a book's page, margins are always folded into the heart.

Our 25th anniversary anthology is divided into *Root, Limb*, and *Tongue*. The metaphors are corporeal and botanical. They are grounded in the soil of Affrilachia. They sprout from that earth and grow large and strong and the limbs leaf out and the canopy casts shade and provides harbor for many. And from that rootedness and that harbor these metaphors speak out. Another way to think about this is that home and history pull up nutrients into the trunk and limb of story and identity and unfurl into the tongue of prophet and witness.

But, as can be seen in the poems of the founding members collected in *Root* (those of Finney, Walker, Wilkinson, Ricardo Nazario y Colón, Norman Ellis, and Coleman), to tell stories grounded in the life and experience of poets born and raised in Affrilachia is to also write a poetry of witness, to engage in the prophetic act of naming and claiming identity and place. Thus, prophecy creates room for spaces that challenge exclusionary narratives, welcomes and provides shelter for all those forced to wander through space, time, and cultures. From the *Root*, grows the *Limb*. And these poems, like those of Quintos, Hagan, Priest, Wilson still explore and address Affrilachia's multiple identities. The question of who we are and how we move through the spaces where we find ourselves is perennial. The poems in Limb branch out into stories of family, into history,and into how identity and politics are always bound up together.

Limbs, in turn grow up and out, they split and divide and unfurl into leaves, and leaves, like tongues rustle and whisper. The poems collected in *Tongue*, are deeply rooted to place and identity, like the poems before, but they are explicitly aware that poetry is by nature political. They are poems that contest and speak back to power. But they also affirm and speak consolation. And, lest readers fall into the trap of thinking that all politics have to do with Black/White relations, oppression, resistance, etc. the poems in *Tongue* have multiple audiences. Indeed, some are to and for each other and are happily unconcerned about speaking to a larger public.

There is so much about this family of writers and artists, activists and educators, that we cannot show you through this collection. We cannot show you how we've watched one another's children grow up—call them niece and nephew. How we smack-talk, laugh hard, turn up the music, clink mason jars, and love one another the hardest through every trial and triumph. How we mourn each other's tragedies. Crow over one another's successes. How *somebody* will have a hand outstretched to welcome you home, no matter how long you've been gone. How we won't ever quit you. We can't recreate the last twenty-five years of family in a literal sense, but it is our hope that you get a feel for it anyway. This anthology is the closest thing we can offer to what it's like being along for the ride on an Affrilachian road-trip, or at a reading, or in someone's living room late at night. It's the closest thing we can offer to welcoming you into the fold. It is our way of saying, you, like we, are travelers, pull up a chair, raise a glass, tell us your story.

Root

PAUL C. TAYLOR

Call Me Out My Name: Inventing Affrilachia

I.

I am grateful for, and humbled by, the opportunity to participate in this symposium on Affrilachia,[1] for reasons both personal and professional. The personal reasons derive from facts like these: I was born and raised in Chattanooga, Tennessee; I spent two years teaching in Lexington, Kentucky, learning from the Affrilachian Poets that my roots in and routes through Appalachia might mean something worth reflecting on; and I come to you now from Centre County, Pennsylvania, in the upper reaches of the region. Like many of the other symposium participants, I am a living testament to the remarkable diversity, racial and otherwise, of Appalachia. Realizing this has been one of the important developments in my life, and I am glad to be in a position to say this publicly.

The professional reasons for my gratitude derive from facts like these: I am working on a book on Black Aesthetics, which means that I get paid to think about things like Affrilachian Poets, and about the conditions that call them into being, and about what they mean and do once they come into being. It is one thing, though, to think about black aesthetics, and another thing entirely to think about the concept at the heart of a particular *venture* in black aesthetics, while in the presence of the people who inaugurated and sustained the venture. My aim here is to do the second thing, albeit briefly: to think through the meaning of Affrilachia from the perspective of black aesthetics, and to do so in the home and in the presence of the Affrilachian Poets. Perhaps specifying the context in this way will clarify my feelings of gratitude and humility.

---

1. http://www.as.uky.edu/academics/departments_programs/IDP/IDP/Africana/Conference/Pages/default.aspx

2.

We have Frank X Walker to thank for the word 'Affrilachia', and for his tireless work in support of the ideas and commitments that the word carries in its train. Walker's journal, *pluck!*, declares the most central of these commitments quite clearly in its mission statement. The journal aims, it says, at "making the invisible visible," which is to say, at showing that Appalachia is more than the lily-white, seamlessly rural home of Lil' Abner and Jed Clampett.

This common picture of Appalachia is already too simple, even before we reach the question of blackness. It obscures, among other things, the complexities that attend the various modes of racialization into whiteness. (I don't have space here to explore this thought any further, so I'll just point to the remarkable television series "Justified," currently running on FX, and move on.) But the standard image of Appalachia probably works hardest at obscuring the presence, plurality, and perspectives of black folks in the region. This is what *pluck!* aims most assiduously to contest.

Putting the concern that animates *pluck!* in terms of invisibility will put most people immediately in mind of Ralph Ellison, whose *Invisible Man* established the problematic of black invisibility in the forms that most of us know best. To be invisible in this sense is a matter not of physics or physiology, of bent light waves or of impaired optical faculties. It is a matter of psychology and morals: it is a matter of what philosophers call recognition, of being regarded as a person, as someone with a moral status and a point of view: someone whose presence makes a difference worth attending to.

The rhetoric of invisibility has served well in this capacity for a long time, appearing before Ellison in the work of Du Bois and others, and well afterwards in, for example, the work of Michele Wallace. (There may, in fact, be no better précis of the dialectic of recognition than Du Bois's discussion of 'seeing oneself through the eyes of others' in his account of double-consciousness.) But focusing on the philosophical problematic behind the ocular metaphors points beyond the metaphor, and invites us to consider other sensory and experiential registers.

When Ellison's narrator bumps into the uncomprehending—the vehemently uncomprehending—white man, he says that the man called him 'an insulting name.' It's not hard to imagine what that name was, especially if one has read Fanon. ("Look, a Negro! Or, more simply: Dirty nigger!") And once we imagine this, it is easy to see that the de-personalization and sub-personalization that constitute invisibility go hand in hand with denying the individuality that we signify with names and titles. (Not 'Excuse me, sir,' but 'Dirty nigger!')

This link between invisibility, recognition, and naming is what makes Sidney Poitier say, 'Call me 'Mr. Tibbs.' It helped motivate the famous signs from the Memphis sanitation workers' strike, the ones that, as the great contemporary artist Glenn Ligon reminds us, read, 'I AM A MAN.' It drove my mother to insist, in the early seventies (back when they still talked this way), that white salesclerks call her 'Mrs. Taylor' rather than 'honey' or 'dear.' To insist in these ways on just these modes of address is to say that *there is a name for what I am, for the kind of thing, the kind of creature, the kind of being, that I am.* It is to say further that I will insist on this name, and demand that you resist your impulse to call me otherwise. I am not a boy, or a beast of burden, or a piece of property, or the object of your condescendingly feigned and double-edged familiarity. I have a name that accurately and appropriately identifies me, and insisting on it is my prerogative and duty in a properly arranged scheme of social relationships.

The invention of the term 'Affrilachia' must, it seems to me, be seen in this context. Invisibility, with its links to naming and recognition, is one of the central tropes in the black aesthetic tradition, as I understand it. It is just one of the central tropes, of course, alongside reflections on beauty and the black body (think of Morrison's *The Bluest Eye*, or of there being no Black Miss Americas until—forgive the expression—high-yellow Vanessa Williams), on authenticity (think of Jean Toomer, or of Dave Chappelle making fun of Wayne Brady, and of Wayne Brady joining him), on the role of politics in art (think of Du Bois and Locke arguing about propaganda, and of Maulana Karenga wondering what in the world there was to argue about), and on the meaning of style (think of flashy white basketball players nicknamed 'white chocolate,' and of what people once called 'blue eyed soul' but now call 'Robin Thicke'). Nevertheless, invisibility may be the most prominent trope, not least because Ellison's novel quickly became and, as far as I know, remains required reading for US high schoolers.

3.

To conjure up a term like 'Affrilachia' is to build on and advance this campaign for visibility. Names and contests over naming are part of the ethical and existential machinery of intersubjective recognition. And black expressive culture has from its very beginnings taken on the task of manipulating this machinery. The standard image of Appalachia results in what one writer refers to, in another context, as metaphysical genocide: it notionally erases Black folks from a sprawling region of 200,000 square miles of land, covering parts of twelve states and all of a thirteenth. Insisting on the black presence in Appalachia, on the existence and vitality of *Affrilachia*, is a way of showing that we are here, of showing ourselves as much as anyone else. It is a way of saying what Larry Neal wrote in his review of *Invisible Man*: we are *not* invisible—at least, *not to each other*.

'Going Up' with the Affrilachian Poets: Birthing (Folk)lore in the MLK Elevator

The Ground Floor:

In the late 1980s and early 1990s, a group of young writers at the University of Kentucky (UK) birthed a collective known as the Affrilachian Poets in the back room of Martin Luther King Cultural Center of the UK. Their story is told by several writers (see Spriggs; Norman; and Newberry) and in the documentary Coal Black Voices. The group formed from a bond of friendship and a love of writing, and got their name largely from the creative power of Frank X Walker who imagined the word "Affrilachia" (now defined in the *Encyclopedia of Appalachia* and the *New Oxford American Dictionary*) into being in those early years. To date, the group is composed of around forty members; founding members include (and here the sources vary; my source coming from a website for the Affrilachian Poets): Frank X Walker, Gerald Coleman, Kelly Norman Ellis, Ricardo Nazario y Colón, Nikky Finney, Mitchell L.H. Douglas, Daundra La'Trice Logan, Crystal Wilkinson, Bernard Clay, and Thomas Aaron.

This essay is interested in focusing on one moment (or set of moments) during the early days of the Affrilachian Poets, what many founding members often refer to as "the elevator days." It is a work to document those moments, those elevator days, in much more detail than they have yet been written about. It also looks to folklore scholarship and views the elevator days and their celebration in various publications and my interviews as a piece of (folk)lore about this writing collective. Before conducting interviews for this essay, my understanding of the elevator days was simple: people went into an elevator, hit the stop button, and share freshly minted original poetry. I'm not sure whether I first heard about these moments in *Coal Black Voices* or in interviews I conducted with Crystal Wilkinson and Gerald Coleman in 2013, but I know that my interest was elevated when I did hear about this intimate poetry space.

2nd Floor, Methods:

I am in contact with many of the Affrilachian Poets. I gained this connection through a relationship with Frank X Walker, which began in 2009 when Dr. Bruce Dick of the English Department at Appalachian State University (ASU) invited me to join him to interview Walker for the *Appalachian Journal*; the interview was published in Volume 38 Number 4, Summer 2011, titled "'Still Chasing These Words': A Conversation with Frank X Walker." Having this connection, I could reach out to members who I knew had taken part in the elevator days: Frank X Walker, Ricardo Nazario y Colón, and Gerald Coleman.

I sent messages on Facebook to each and asked if I could interview them through Skype, a phone call, or email. In less than a day they all agreed to talk with me. We set up times to talk: a Skype conversation with Ricardo Nazario y Colón, a phone call with Coleman, and an email with Walker. I knew going into these interviews that I would be using a snowball method of collecting the names of people I needed to talk to. I also had a list of prepared questions, so that each interview would follow a fairly standard model of a semi-structured interview, allowing room to deviate from my questions if needed. From my interviews, I was told to reach out to Kelly Norman Ellis, Miysan Crosswhite, Jude McPherson, Paul C. Taylor, Mitchell L.H. Douglas, Shana Smith, and Daundra La'Trice Logan; I did so, but was only able to interview Crosswhite on the phone, and McPherson through email, who replied that he had come into the group after the elevator days.

Out of this group I conducted four interviews. Walker's was documented through his response to my email, and the other three were recorded on an audio recorder. Nazario-Colón's lasted about thirty minutes, Coleman's closer to an hour, and Crosswhite's under thirty minutes. I transcribed all of Ricardo Nazario y Colón, and portions of Coleman's and Crosswhite's.

3rd Floor, Lit Review:

To focus a bit more in the realm of folklore, we will look to the elevator days as an example of folklore customs, described in Jan Harold Brunvand's *The Study of American Folklore* as "a traditional *practice*—a mode of individual behavior or a habit of social life—transmitted by word of mouth or imitation, then ingrained by social pressure, common usage, and parental or other authority" (406). In relation the interviews, it becomes apparent how the elevator days can be seen as a folklore custom.

Turning to the first page of Jan Harold Brunvand's *The Study of American Folklore*, we read: first the question "WHAT IS FOLKLORE," and then the answer that "[F]olklore comprises the unrecorded traditions of a people" (3). Taken at that basic level, this project is ninety-nine percent folklore; ninety-nine percent, because in documenting the writers' own stories about their elevator days, their largely "unrecorded traditions" have become recorded. To my knowledge, this subject has not yet been thoroughly documented and is but briefly mentioned in a few places, as we will see later in this essay.

Brunvand continues, "[T]he study of folklore…records and attempts to analyze these traditions…so as to reveal the common life of the human mind apart from what is contained in the formal records of culture that compose the heritage of a people" (3). Again, this project is documenting a largely un-recorded set of moments in the earliest days of the Affrilachian Poets, in a piece of their heritage/lore. Brunvand also quotes Archer Taylor— "[O]ne of the greatest folklorists of his generation" (Goldberg 704)—who says, "[F]olklore is the material that is handed on by tradition, either by word of mouth or custom and practice" (5). The "material" is the stories of the elevator days, and while it has sparsely been "handed on by tradition," there exist interesting ways in which some of the Affrilachian Poets, and others, keep these moments alive by talking about them.

Brunvand gives this essay more room in folklore circles where he writes, "[F]olklore is traditional in two senses in that it is passed on repeatedly in a relatively fixed or standard form, and it circulates among members of a particular group" (12). No, the elevator days don't seem to be getting "passed on repeatedly," but the ways they are talked about do come "in a relatively fixed or standard form"; and there is no argument that the only people talking about the elevator days are either members of the Affrilachian Poets or friends, fans, and scholars of the Affrilachian Poets. Brunvand's next sentence becomes critical to this research. He explains that

> Traditional form or structures allows us to recognize corresponding bits of folklore in different guises. The characters in a story, the setting, the length, the style, even the language may vary, but we can still call it the "same" story if it maintains a basic underlying form. (12)

While my interviews revealed details to my original understanding of the elevator days, they still maintained "a basic underlying form" of poets reading poems in an elevator.

In addition to looking at Brunvand's definitions of folklore, I turn to the personal-experience story/narrative (PEN), which ebbs in and out of traditional folklore studies in much the same way I've said the elevator days do. Sandra Dolby writes in *American Folklore: An Encyclopedia* that a PEN is

> usually told in the first person, and [contains] nontraditional content. Unlike most folklore, a personal-experience story is not passed down through time and space and kept alive through variation from one teller to another. Instead, the content of a personal-experience story is based on an actual event in the life of a storyteller. (556–557)

In looking at my interviews, we will see how the elevator days flow in and out of a PEN just as they do in traditional folklore. The interviews are told in first person, and in some regards they do contain "nontraditional content," but the story has been "passed down through time and space," and is "[being] kept alive through variation from one teller to another"; as well as through non-Affrilachian Poets writing about the elevator days (including myself).

Dolby also makes the claim that "such stories do not enter tradition" (557). But as alluded to, mention of the elevator days has cropped up in several places. Kelly Norman Ellis, Frank X Walker, and Ricardo Nazario y Colón all talk about the elevator days in *Coal Black Voices*. Ellis starts off discussing her introduction to the Affrilachian Poets, and then mentions, "I didn't know at the time about Frank and Ricardo meeting in the elevators." Her saying "I didn't know at the time," at least to me, creates a tradition, a (folk)lore, out of these experiences. Something happened important enough for her to need to know about, and to talk about after she learned.

After Ellis mentions "Frank and Ricardo meeting in the elevators," the film shifts to an animated Ricardo Nazario y Colón. He speaks to the elevator days, explaining, "[T]he elevator seemed like the right place. Maybe fifty feet from the cultural center. Close enough to make us feel safe and be able to share what we wanted to share, and feel good about. And then just come out [of the elevator] like nothing happened." The film moves to Walker who, with a grin on his face, says, "We'd actually go into the elevator, close it, and then cut the power off, and have these real quiet poetry sharings in private, in the elevator."

As mentioned earlier in this essay, both Gerald Coleman and Crystal Wilkinson talked to me briefly about the elevator days in personal interviews conducted in the fall of 2013. What is perhaps more interesting, though, is Gurney Norman's commentary in an issue of Iron Mountain Review on Frank X Walker. Norman, a previous Poet Laureate of Kentucky, recipient of a National Book Award for his novel Divine Right's Trip (1972), long-time English professor at the University of Kentucky, and mentor and publisher of Walker's since 1981 (Norman 26–27), has a connection and history with the Affrilachian Poets (Garrison 1078–1079). Perhaps this connection gave him the insight to mention the elevator days in his piece, "Affrilachian Genesis." He writes of first being presented with the word "Affrilachia" through Walker's poem, "Affrialchia," and then says,

> In the following months, I became aware of a new literary group in Lexington called the Affrilachian Poets. Frank's word had called into being a dynamic group of young African American writers, most of them from Kentucky but not all. Some of their antics included crowding into an elevator in our tallest building on campus and writing quick poems as the elevator rose to the eighteenth floor. (26)

A good deal of what Norman writes is slightly off from the stories I have heard, of discussions about who and how the Affrilachian Poets formed, and how the word "Affrilachia" played into "[calling] into being" the Affrilachian Poets. Mainly, the issue being that at least Walker, Coleman, Ricardo Nazario y Colón, and Ellis were friends and writing together before Walker invented the word "Affrilachia." In talking about the earliest days of the Affrilachian Poets, Coleman told me, "even before we put a name on it, it was just a group of poets. You're only talking about five, six, seven people." It seems Frank is perhaps becoming a Jack figure in his larger than life (or best-son/poet) status.

More importantly for this essay, Norman gets a bit creative in his description of the "antics" of the Affrilachian Poets. From my interviews, I got more details about the space the elevator days took place in. The building the elevator days took place in (the Student Center at UK) was only three stories high. So, when I reread this piece after my interviews, I questioned whether Norman was taking what he had heard from the group and adding his own details (as writers are wont to do), or if he was telling his readers about another (unheard of) example of the elevator days. Curious about this story, I first contacted Ricardo Nazario y Colón and Coleman who both told me to ask Walker and Ellis. I sent Walker an email, asking "Did this happen, or is [Norman] telling Wilgus stories" (Wilgus being a fictional character in *Norman's Kinfolks: The Wilgus Stories* and *Ancient Creek*). Walker's response was quick, and reads, "Gurney told a Wilgus story."

There is much to say about Norman's "Wilgus story" here, like how it shows variation in a tradition, a piece of the Affrilachian Poet's lore being circulated by a friend of the Affrilachian Poets (and who I know I read somewhere, I just can't remember where, was made an honorary Affrilachian Poet by Walker—or perhaps I'm creating my own folklore about the group and Gurney Norman here…). The most important thing to say here, though, is that Gurney Norman has just told a tale on the Affrilachian Poets. In telling this tale, he adds, significantly, to the (folk)lore of the Affrilachian Poets.

4th Floor, Interviews:

Here I will look to certain responses from my four interviewees: Gerald Coleman, Miysan Crosswhite, Ricardo Nazario y Colón, and Frank X Walker. I won't go into every question I asked, nor every answer I received, but instead will try and focus on the more important aspects of their recollections of the elevator days. My main goal is to detail what happened, how it started, why the elevator, and then to look to some intriguing responses from my interviewees. Going into these interviews, and especially my first one with Nazario-Colòn, I was expecting to find deviations from each of my participants, which I did.

I'll begin with how they started reading poetry in an elevator. Both Nazario y Colón and Crosswhite talk about how people would show up at the Martin Luther King Cultural/ Student Center—Crosswhite says with a "smile on their face…that look [that they have new poetry to share]"—and that they would go into the elevator and have a "poetry moment" (Coleman; Nazario y Colón). Coleman, however, remembers these moments in greater detail, and adds to the story of how they first thought to get in the elevator (see his interview in Appendix B for some of the detail of the physical space in the MLK Cultural Center at the UK). He states, "[S]o the first stop was always the back office in the cultural center. That's really where we would go. And you would go back there and close the door." Crosswhite mentions how "the MLK Center was always so busy," and then says, "[W]hen you had the office doors maybe closed, where the back office was, people would still come in and they might interrupt the flow of what you were trying to bring across, or read at that time. So, the elevator was, it was quiet." Unlike Coleman, however, Crosswhite doesn't explicitly state that poems were first read in this room and that the elevator became a secondary spot.

Coleman leads us through the MLK Cultural Center from an occupied back office, to the second and third floors of the center, and, he explains, "eventually, it was like, 'okay, where do we go?' And…a couple of us were on the elevator one day… And one of us, just, when the doors were closed, pulled the elevator stop button." From these three responses we find variation: Ricardo Nazario y Colón goes right into the elevator, as does Crosswhite in a way while hinting at a crowded back office in the MLK Center as the reason for getting the elevator, and Coleman laying it all out, from the earliest moments in the back office to a need for a quiet space, found in the elevator. Walker's answer is probably the shortest of all (and granted, all of his were short due to the difference in his interview through email, and the others by phone and Skype). He writes, "Prior to the moment, someone would covertly signal those in the know that a moment was imminent and available individuals would casually leave a crowded King Center and reassemble in or near the elevator."

Something important to discuss that we see each of my participants mention is the phrase, "poetry moment." Going into these interviews, I was unsure exactly what happened when they got in the elevator and hit the stop button. I knew poetry was read, but I wasn't sure if this was a workshop moment or something else. Here all my participants talked about how the main use of this elevators was to have a "poetry moment." Coleman defined these moments saying,

> I think the important part to remember is why we called it a poetry moment, because I can see how that would seem off to people looking at it from the outside. That, okay, you have somebody read a poem and then they kind of look at each other and walk off. Nobody really said anything…For us, it was a moment. A moment in time that we filled with poetry, and you didn't sully that moment by trying to turn it into a mini-workshop.

Walker and Nazario y Colón second Coleman, affirming that these moments were just that, moments and not workshops. Crosswhite, however, remembers differently, telling me, "it became that moment, kind of a workshop moment." I would question his recollection if it weren't for something Coleman told me: "I know there were times when people had moments and I wasn't on the elevator." So it's possible that Crosswhite was on the elevator a time, or many times, with people other than Coleman, Walker, and Nazario y Colón, and where Crosswhite and others did workshop poetry.

I also tried to find out who may have been the first person to stop the elevator. As with most of my questions, I received a range of answers. However, with this particular question, the answers ranged from people to people, and in rather amusing ways. Both Nazario y Colón and Walker told me it was likely Coleman. And then Nazario y Colón also says, "Usually things like these, probably [it] is like the least [likely] person, the person that you think would not have come up with it. So I'm going to say Thomas Aaron came up with the idea." And then we get Crosswhite and Coleman's responses, which add humor and depth to the elevator lore.

At first Coleman says, "[E]ither me and Ricardo, or me and Frank." But then he adds,

> probably not Frank, because he was directing the culture center…So it was either me, or it was Ricardo, and Ricardo just doesn't remember it was him, or doesn't want to fess up to the fact that it was him. We may both have decided in the back of our minds back then that we didn't want to be blamed for being the ones who did. So, it was very likely Ricardo and I.

Crosswhite had a similar response, only shorter: "I would say it was more than likely Ricardo, because he was the one who was the craziest one out of us."

Something else I received varying responses on was whether anyone ever got caught, or got in trouble, from hitting the stop button on the elevator. None of my interviewees mentioned being disciplined, but some said there was an alarm and others said there was no alarm. Both Coleman and Crosswhite said that they were never caught, and never "reprimanded" (Crosswhite). Coleman elaborates, saying,

> And one of us, just when the doors were closed, pulled the elevator stop button. And it just so happened, for whatever reason, they either hadn't installed an alarm…or it just wasn't' working. Whatever the case was,

whenever you pulled that little stop button, the elevator would stop between floors but no alarm would sound. It would just sit there. And the other thing that kind of made us think it was alright to get away with that, no one ever used that elevator. That was the least used elevator I have ever seen in my life, because it was right next to the stairwell that was just kind of a, it was a three-flight stairwell. But most people were either going to the first floor, where we already were, or the second floor.

However, Nazario y Colón told me that when they hit the stop button an alarm would sound. He added,

> The times I went in, the custodians knew. We knew them. And we would come out the elevator, they'd be looking at us. We'd be like, "oh, we're good now." They would laugh, and you know, that kind of thing. They only responded because the building manager wanted to make sure that someone wasn't really trapped in there. Nobody's rushing to the elevator to rescue anybody.

Again, Walker's responses were brief, but still informative. He told me about getting caught: "Occasionally, we'd get caught. Never in trouble." This tells me that he too remembers an alarm sounding, or at least getting caught for being on the elevator in a three-floor building for such a long time.

One question I asked that provided surprising responses (a bit more than others) was whether they wanted to stop elevators when they get in them today. I expected everyone to say, "of course," because, personally, I think the elevator days are such a special thing they all experienced—experienced, in the past tense, as it doesn't seem the elevator days are (as) alive as they were. Nazario y Colón laughed at first, then told me, "No," laughed some more, and continued, "No. You know, that's a good idea. I have not done that. Maybe I just sat in the elevator without having to pull the switch." Walker says, "Actually, no." Coleman's response was shorter than most of his answers, and like Nazario-Colòn, he laughed at first: "I don't get on elevators that much. So, you know. But I wouldn't be surprised if some of us have a moment every now and then when we have that little flashback." Crosswhite, amused along with Nazario y Colón and Coleman, said, "Oh, man, that would be awesome…There's moments." And then he told me about getting trapped on an elevator a few years ago, saying of the moment, "I was like, wow, this would be a great Affrilachian moment."

To go back to Coleman's response—"I wouldn't be surprised if some of us have a moment every now and then"—Nazario y Colón first said no, and then had an aha! moment about the Affrilachian Poets' fifteenth anniversary. He remembers that a group "went to UK because I worked at UK, so I had keys. And we went, and we got in the elevator. And Amanda Johnston was in the elevator. Parneshia Jones. Frank. Myself. And we had a quick moment. And Gerald. And Gerald, yeah."

This brings me to the last part of my interviews, which is asking why the elevator days stopped. Crosswhite told me that as the group grew it became too big, had too many members, to have these elevator moments. Nazario y Colón, however, said it was likely because people were graduating and leaving the UK: "you know, kind of the energy, that core group, was just beginning to go in other different directions." Coleman had a similar answer, though in different words and an interesting metaphor. He told me, "It's hard to pinpoint. It's kind of like a festival. If you have a three day festival, some people get there on Friday and leave on Saturday. Some people come Saturday and stay till Sunday. Some come Friday night, leave Saturday morning. You know what I mean? People were coming in and going out."

A core belief here, regardless of the different responses, is an end to the elevator days. Walker gave me a much different answer, though. He writes, "Not sure that is has stopped." It comes to mind as I sit here at my desk writing that Walker is the only one of my four interviewees who still works at the UK. Crosswhite lives in Mobile, Alabama; Coleman in Atlanta, Georgia; and Nazario y Colón not far from Walker near Morehead, Kentucky. Maybe Walker knows something the others don't know. Or maybe he just has more hope. Or maybe he's telling Wilgus stories, unwilling to divulge all of the elevator's secrets. Whatever it is, if we go back to Crosswhite's *moment* and Nazario y Colón remembering about the Affrilachian Poets' fifteenth anniversary, and add Walker's statement, "[N]ot sure that it has stopped," we've got folklore. We've got a continuation of a customary practice of the Affrilachian Poets, and a way of seeing these past moments as not over, as possible in the future.

Rooftop, The End?:
To close, let us first go back, back to Brunvand on folkore:

> Traditional form or structures allows us to recognize corresponding bits of folklore in different guises. The characters in a story, the setting, the length, the style, even the language may vary, but we can still call it the "same" story if it maintains a basic underlying form. (12)

Here the elevator days, these poetry moments, seen in a different guise than a Jack Tale, for instance, can be looked at as folklore of the Affrilachian Poets. More specifically, in this brief analysis using aspects of folklore and PENs, we can say firmly that the elevator days are a piece of folklore about the earliest days of the Affrilachian Poets. Certain aspects can be applied to the PEN, but I see more of a relationship to folklore, especially when we consider the continuation of the elevator days if not in practice, then at least in stories told about them, and how the stories/interviews I have discussed here have a "basic underlying form." In random occurrences, such as getting stuck on elevators, anniversary moments, and that day I find an elevator with a stop button I can push, and a poem I can read, the elevator days have entered into the folklore of the Affrilachian Poets.

Works Cited

Brunvand, Jon Harold. ""The Field Of Folklore." *The Study of American Folklore: An Introduction (Fourth Edition)*. New York: W.W. Norton & Company, 1998: 3–21.

Coleman, Gerald. Personal Interview. 19 Mar. 2015. Audio File.

Crosswhite, Miysan. Personal Interview. 9 Apr. 2015. Audio file.

Dolby, Sandra. "Personal-Experience Story." *American Folklore: An Encyclopedia*. Ed. Jan Harold Brunvand. New York: Garland, 1998: 556–558.

Donohue, Jean, Fred Johnson, Gurney Norman, and C D. Dawson. *Coal Black Voices*. Covington, KY: Media Working Group, 2006.

Garrison, Andrew. "Norman, Gurney." *Encyclopedia of Appalachia*. Eds. Rudy Abramson and Jean Haskell. Knoxville: The U of Tennessee P, 2006: 1078–1079.

Goldberg, Christine. "Taylor, Archer (1890–1973)." *American Folklore: An Encyclopedia*. Ed. Jan Harold Brunvand. New York: Garland, 1998: 704–705.

Nazario y Colón, Ricardo. Personal Interview. 16 Mar. 2015. Typed transcript.

Newberry, Elizabeth R. "Affrilachians." *Encyclopedia of Appalachia*. Eds. Rudy Abramson and Jean Haskell. Knoxville: The U of Tennessee P, 2006. 246.

Norman, Gurney. "Affrilachian Genesis." *Iron Mountain Review* 25 (Spring 2009): 26–27.

Spriggs, Bianca. "Frank X Walker: Exemplar of Affrilachia." *Appalachian Heritage* 39.4 (Fall 2011): 21–25.

Walker, Frank X. Personal Interview. 24 Mar. 2015. Email.

FRANK X WALKER

Affrilachia

for Gurney and Anne

thoroughbred racing
and hee haw
are burdensome images
for Kentucky sons
venturing beyond the mason-dixon

anywhere in Appalachia
is about as far
as you could get
from our house
in the projects
yet
a mutual appreciation
for fresh greens
and cornbread
an almost heroic notion
of family
and porches
makes us kinfolk
somehow
but having never ridden
bareback
or sidesaddle

and being inexperienced
at cutting
hanging
or chewing tobacco
yet still feeling
complete and proud to say
that some of the bluegrass
is black
enough to know
that being 'colored' and all
is generally lost
somewhere between
the dukes of hazard
and the beverly hillbillies

but
if you think
makin,'shine from corn
is as hard as Kentucky coal
imagine being
an Affrilachian
poet

Affrilachian MixTape I: Turntablism

Did you get born to John Henry's
body breaking
on flat beds and rifle racks?
Is your blues Stamp Paid's
row
to the   free   side
or the funk of pig feet or the tighten up
from Deweese Street
to
De
troit?

Did you get down on the Cumberland's
birthwater
or grits with sugar not
pepper
or the steel mills of Homewood?
Does you Affrilachian mix
scratch Curtis Mayfield
on vinyl
to do-ragged men who hate
the bony spine of mountain holding
them prisoner?

Holla if you
Holla if
Holla if you hear
the black banjo

And what of a Wheeling beat box
of genuine negro jigs
and maybe
Dixie is a black
song?
And what if
a doe see doe
Virginia reel
and Tennessee waltz
was born from black juba?

                Ain't no sunshine when she's gone

Keep time people.
Keep
time.

Like a rustle of ankle chains
and conga,
mariachi is the new
jam

This is Affrilachian turn
tablism

Holla if you hear
Holla if you
here.

GERALD L. COLEMAN

bless your heart

i don't remember
where i heard it
first
it was just
in the air
like please, thank you
and ma'am

it's that tart
piece of lemon
floating on a
white frosty layer
of glaze
in the sweet ice tea
it's that extra inch
of meringue
on the brown
sugar pie
it was the big smile
wrapped around
a cruel lie

you see, down here
where the ale eight is cold
and the a la mode is warm

where cole slaw
and baked beans
on the side
of fried catfish
is the law
we don't scream
kiss my ass

we like to pour molasses
on our consternation
lap it up
with a biscuit

nobody does it better
than a saccharine
sanguine sara
a how do you do
sally mae, anna bell
patricia faye or abbie gail
with her gum poppin
and her hips rockin
to the side
with a manicured hand
perched
just so
on a hip
curved like a
granny smith apple

you see, down this way
where the grass
is blue

between the corn bread
and the corn puddin
with homemade rolls
and collard greens
chased down with
five
berry
pie
we don't holla
dumb motherfucker or
take the lord's name
in vain

we like to spread butter
all over our dissatisfaction
eat it toasted
maybe with a little
jam

so listen close
or you might
mistake the smile
for a grin
or the curse
for a blessing

because
down here
where the whisky
is bourbon
and the koolaid
is diabetes sweet

we don't yell
fuck you

we like to smother it
and cover it
with gravy
until it's running
over the sides

down here
we smile
we wave
and say

bless your heart

Brown Country

Why certainly I loves country
am partial to a sad sappy love song
and head back howling for a lost love
I live to the tune of hoping hopelessly
I am country
and drawn to the music of the land
not the red on the white in the blue
but the green and the amber
and the ochre-orange country
Natively black foot
with land earth ocean
where fathers and their mothers smoldered
in the name of the Union
how come ain't no sad country songs
about Indians being holocausted
or Africans jumping the broom on Sundays
for to never see their Sweety again
When it's only me
I turn the car radio to it
the spot where God-Family-Country live
polygamously
through the silence a voice laughs asking
"You ain't really gonna listen to that are you?"
Yeah Good Buddy I'm listening

so let the chips fall where they may
Because I do
do so love the brown and the black
of the red on the white in the blue

Does loving country and craving a song
that brings my own black-balled eyes
up to the depth of my haunted-hunted heart
does that make me a country music fan
a natural for sorrow
a Charlene Pride of poetry
a black country singer
with acoustic and eraser
plucking a nappy live wire

I who sing along with the twanging
of the car radio
with country songs
when nobody is listening
how do you explain being African
and loving country
not the red or the white in the blue
but the green and the amber and the ochre-orange
You never explain
just let the good times roll

Carolina born
so I seen it all
from sea to shining sea island
I play it back to you
with a pencil sharp guitar
and hambone hard with the other

I come backed by fiddle and calypso
And on certain notes
my gullah starts to drawl

Mercy Me
I'll throw my head back in a minute
even close my eyes tight when I sing
it's always something about losing my head
or making up with
Or just plain wallowing in the pain of love
Awww come on now
You know how it goes

I'm no Dolly or Billy Ray
But I sho am country

And when I'm gone
Please somebody feed my cat
and in return I'll make my voice
low country quiver real good
then roll for you
you laughing but
this really ain't nothing "shakey bakey"
cause I know folks born in a Holler
who scream all their life
and nobody ever writes a song about them
shouldn't that be a country's song too
or is that only poverty
and the private property of Bluesmen
and Plumbleached women
another jurisdiction
another country

At the end of my singing
it's always so Grand Old Oprey hot
that my mascara's usually running
and by then the Breck hairspray
has wilted my locks
back to lion size normal
and I'm ready to unhitch my silver buckle
drop my jean skirt to the floor
and find me some indigo
to wrap back around my waist

WellShootGoodBuddy
what more do I have to do to prove it
I tell you it's true I am a black country singer
Cause what there is for me to sing about
Should make you push your beer to the side
and take a walk through some
Black family farm land some
Black burial grounds
now sold and desecrated
by golf ball signs that say 'Private Drive'
should make you want to know
this singing southerner's truth
it's my job living in this brown country
to take you inside of real live heartache
and make you tap your foot long enough
and make you smile at yourself
until you recognize your Daddy's face floating
in what I'm saying

Until you ask yourself
as you walk away

does she really listen to Country music
or was that just a poem

Oh why am I fooling myself
They won't never say
I ever sang a good country song
I'm the wrong shade of country
They'll just be mad
that I never let you forget for one minute
that country, the land, is color coded
and that country, the music, is pretty shady too

Country
the twanging one you always hear
is sometimes sad
but always sweet
steeped in honor and family
and cheating checkered skirts
and the backside of some poor slithering creature
pummeled and stretched
into a pair of roach killing boots
they dance to the sizzling notes that
I just lean and listen to
the long and lazy stretched out lines
about life
but whose life
and whose country

This is not about happy endings
this music ain't concerning Cinderellas
but stepsisters and sons and pumpkins
and shoes that never fit some feet

and the lonely of life
and how dance it back away
so why does
this Black girl's iambic feet
always have to doe-see-doe in your face about it
why does she have to sing country music
to herself
along in her car to not be afraid
why can't she buy a front row seat
and wave to Naomi Judd
singing those too close to Aretha like lines
"I love you so stinking much that
if you ever try and leave me I'm with you"

I love country
for the tender story
for the blazing heart
for the ache and sorrow sweetness
that is always there
for the green in the amber of the ochre-orange
in the red on the white of the blue
that I always feel

Oh what the hell
I am country I like
listening to its sweet tang
linger like a sour apple
baked to the pipes of my roasted mouth

As I drive this back road
I take taste of it
as I pull into this honkey tonk gas station

and pump 5 dollars premium
I sing along until
I hear my radio's same song even louder now
and look around for the twin source
rolling out a hiked up summertime window
there in the diner next to the station
I know the words but my daddy's lips freeze
I end my harmless sing-a-long and look up

I fall into dozens of crawling all over me eyes
that accompany the Kentucky Headhunter tune
they are full of catfish and budweiser and quickly
turn into razors swinging in the August air

I feel the blood gushing
cutting the music into
the red then the white the blue of my brown

This place where the cowboy under the hat
spits the color of my mother's skin out his window
I was taught never to step inside
he knows all this an follows my every move
guzzling down his yahoo drink
he brings his buddies to the looking glass
they zip their pants
up and down like a fiddle
as one of them begins to step away from the rest
I need to pay for my gas and go
but my swinging feet are stitched frozen to my lips
I look away to the woods all around
My grandfather is untying himself from all the trees
He pops and stretches his many necks back into place

He steps toward me
He says I should consider history
the payment in full

Country music is historical
This is the music we were lynched by
These are the hangman's songs

Tujcalusa

In the west side of Tujcalusa,
country boys still say howdy and ma'am
and they tip their cowboy hats
to salute a lady.

This morning their daily ritual
was interrupted by a subtle nod
from a vaquero with his family.

The Copenhagen smiles disappeared
and memories of the running of the bull
across the deep South decades ago,
brought about a chill at the country store
we call K-Mart.

Alabama sounds Spanish to me
and Tujcalusa reminds me of Yabucoa,
Humacao and other aboriginal names
in Puerto Rico. The familiarity of these names
beckons me.

But this is the Deep South
and no matter how thirsty you are
or how warm it is outside,
it can be a cold place to take a drink of water.

O Tobacco

You are a Kentucky tiller's livelihood.
You were school clothes in August
the turkey at Thanksgiving
Christmas
with all the trimmings.

I close my eyes
see you tall
stately green
lined up in rows.
See sweat seeping
through Granddaddy's shirt
as he fathered you first.

You were protected by him
sometimes even more
than any other thing
that rooted in our earth.

Just like family you were
coddled
cuddled
coaxed
into making him proud.

Spread out for miles
you were the only
pretty thing
he knew.

When I think of you
at the edge of winter,
I see you, brown, wrinkled
just like Granddaddy's skin.

A ten-year old me
plays in the shadows
of the stripping room
the wood stove burns
calloused hands twist
through the length
of your leaves.
Granddaddy smiles
nods at me when he
thinks I'm not looking.

You are pretty
and braided
lined up in rows
like a room full of
brown girls
with skirts hooped out
for dancing.

Grits

First Published: Duende *Magazine: October 2014*

For the way they stick to all 24 of my ribs, coat & dramatic hold—my god—
I love grits & their salt when I'm done dressing their simple bodies, harmony
Hominy & song For the hot mill & milk & warm they make me

& Chicago Sunday morning w/ garlic & cheese & frozen coke cola that Kelly makes for
Parneshia, baby Naomi & me—in her adopted city before Parneshia
flies me to sky—all morning we are gratify & sate

& Waffle Houses from Lexington, Kentucky to Gulfport, Mississippi, where they
lay slices of American cheese over like prayers, small hell yeses in our bowls—
fried egg sandwiches w/ pickles & coffee, but lord it's the grits, always—

& Magnolias uptown in Charleston w/ David—grits w/ spicy shrimp, sausage
& tasso gravy, we are douse & want—in love & its taste is country & cloy—
all shellfish & corn, all ground & earth

& Clover Grill grits & yolk, buttered biscuits w/ gravy & pork chops, while the grill
sizzles sexy like & we all smell of stale Abita & smoke & the Soul Rebels still revolve &
it's 3am in the Quarter & we all, all of us feel home

& this morning All the silence of a Sunday hot water, ¼ cup meal, cheese, salt,
milk & coffee & this poem & New York can feel South, can make the distance feel
full still & not as bitter as it sometimes—is

SHAYLA LAWSON

THE KENTUCKY–IST

Sammy Davis, Jr., Jr. is the name of my dog.
Yes, this comes from another book. Yes, this is
his officious name because
he reminds me of a spry black Jew. Yes,
this is still racist, even coming from me.

The –ist pulls the best out of all of us.
It is the low-slung onomatopoetic
operatic of the tire swing hung
from my neighbor's tree, *ist*, a red
cable fashioned as a noose. The descendants

of southern transcendentalists,
they will use the same knot come Halloween
(the death man cometh) clinging to the effigies
of tissue ghosts and, come spring,
a basketball coach (the ice man taketh away)—
the satirist—garbage bags clad in suits of papier mâche.

The historicist: because everyone needs
something large and black and fearful hanging
from a beech. *Ist*—The sound wearing wind in its teeth.
Gap-toothed, warden, sneer-sucking tongue—
and that was just the Disney version. Even now, I hear
Cin-cin-NAT-tah, but I see Emmet Till and Sammy

Davis, Jr. [,Sr.] in the golden Cadillac to Kim Novak's
hiding in the backseat. They file by the Volvo
window parked at the Winn-Dixie
My fat adolescent fingers scanning the white sheet
the conic iconic, a family-of-four, in rain-spit grit.

I say, "Mom, it's the Klan." She looks through
the rear view, sucks Maybelline off her teeth before
scrounging her purse for bills,
"Well, you better hurry on in there, then. You
better get on. Those eggs won't buy themselves."

In the City

rear-wheel-drive cuttin co'ners   rims rubbin through the city
fishtail swingin switchin lanes   floatin tub in the city

M-4 extended barrel peeks out from beneath the seat   shit
gotta stay above   the mud in the city

spit-rolled blunts sit coolin in the swivel of air vent   there
for when it starts   the tug of the city

palm the finger waves   her face hidden in the sex of my lap
this how a king fall in love in the city

family heir at age twelve   when pops went to the grave
couldn't find my heart if they dug up the city

mothers shoot brown sugar into the rupture of vein
i live   like this   through the blood of the city

stay glued to the rearview   in a forever state of flight
a bad omen   i am   the black dove of the city

not quite a fiend   just sprinkle a little out the bag
to do a few bumps   just because   in the city

redbone rhythm her first time breaths   only sound
that ever drowned   out the buzz   of the city

now the joy of her moan live ringin   i waste in La Grange
forever reminiscing how it was   in the city

fleur-de-lis

sidney bechet bought an old, beat-up soprano saxophone, when it is difficult enough to play one that's in tune. he was gallant like that; when he was wont, he planted *petite fleur* in quiet imaginations. similar to the way he might enter a blossom, wrap himself in the bouquet, buzz his malediction, and retreat to paris, a pilgrim sets out on a journey to find her holy place, an ice cube wanders discursively along an aqueous path till it has fully realized new liquid form; this i am sure of, if only because i am myself a b7 minor, sanctum, and slowly melting. what line is not after another? what note either in a lucent solo? railroad tracks run from east coast to west coast and back, the train takes the tramp wherever she wants to go. at some point she will find herself along the banks of the ohio in a river city looking for lost treasure—a gold medal tossed into a great waterway by an ex-patriot. the lilies in this city have no sweet odor for they are made iron, and rust with time. the meter also changes—it is in the variation of timing and stress that a feel is created that gets the whole storyville jumping. and while the cathouse wholly throbs with vice, poets make the polite music of the middle class. you can make poetry whorish, but you can't make it unpopular. a breeze stumbles in on this gruesome scene and pets the wilting yellow iris in a vase. she is a flower of basin street, her occupation is to be known, and known often well. why do we try so hard to be beautiful, when we already are? he was rough, and before she knew it was all over, her little flower was gone.

on aging

> *O, for a beaker full of the warm South*
> —John Keats, "Ode to a Nightingale"

a five-story continuous column
       still
rises above a muddy runt of a creek.

                             it is not really snowing,
      the sky is peeling
from its psoriasis. skeletons of various deciduous trees

      resign themselves to the coming of many cold, gray days.
whiskey
is about the only thing   that likes the change
      in season,
the passing of time. white oak from fordsville, ky,

dried and stacked
      to speed maturity, is cut into staves
to form barrels. hungry flames belch out of

these new vessels;
      wood smoke scents the insouciant air. charring,
                            in good time,

makes a whiskey wise, ambers its tone, and gives it its whiskers.
what does it feel like, you ask.
        to be so devoted to darkening i am a sour mash

                        of bleak and garbled omens?
the devil has to get his cut—if we are honest with ourselves,
        we must admit
what unfolds from time cannot be anticipated. the most important thing
is to be open to wonder and surprise—

to the poem. which leads us to georgetown
where the very right reverend elijah craig is supposed
        to have distilled the first whiskey using corn and limestone water

(the master distiller's dream).

 there are two contradictory elements that run through
        american history like the red
and white stripes across old glory: they are stern piety

            and the need to carouse. after just one year of pastoring,
      gray hairs
begin to sprout from around the temples. by the time i married

my first couple,
i looked like i could be their father,
when in truth,
i am just a few years older than them. likewise,
                 the presidency changes a person.

halfway through his first term obama had just a few silvery stragglers,
by the end of his time in office,

it is a snowy evening. the old saying goes,
a little whiskey for the stomach.

but what of the head? the heart? all of those compromises

of your principles
must hasten one's descent
into the grave? in the early aromas

there are no axes of concern. the nose is intensely fruited,

bears a tantalizing citrus zest.
the body is broad, silky,
almost chewable; the palate is tremendously buttery

with some sherry notes,
a dash of dried fruits, and whisper of creamy vanilla. The finish is long
and elegant. these are words of an aesthete

in a feeble attempt to discover
a way to talk
about the taste of taking away a little grace
and hope from each encounter.

then i checked the label
and found that it was 126 proof: when you buy
a fine bourbon,
you're also buying time, and it can fool you. but then,
if you need to erase the rough spots
in an evening,
there's nothing better.

Praisesong for a Mountain

O, mountain,
I am your daughter.

Once, before I knew you,
I mistook you
for a low-hanging thunderhead.

Or thought maybe
you were a blue whale
that had lost its way,
blinded by the sun.

O, mountain,
      linger—
be my whole horizon.

Let me never open
my eyes and see a thing
but your hoary grace.

You are the missing
rib of the Earth.

You are the climax
of a god's birth.

You are the mausoleum
of burnt-out stars.

O, mountain,
I wish one day
to be buried
in your third eye.

Lend me something
of yourself:
your posture,
your grip,
your innermost
jewel-toned seam,
so that I too, may endure.

Black Diamonds

for Mrs. Sweet Genny Lynch

Whatchu know about black diamonds, black diamonds, black diamonds?
Whatchu know about soooul?
Whatcha know about coooal?

Whatchu know about the pressure
of the earth
turning soil to coal
turning coal to diamonds?
They say
they say….one day
millions and millions of years of pressure
       of pressure
       of pressure
form diamonds
in colors: black, pink, yellow, green.

Today, this pressure forms black diamonds
       from blood
       from sweat
       from love
from slaves buried in unmarked graves.

Black diamonds form on days like April 5th 2010.
That day started just like all the other days
just like all the all the days
the other days
the hundreds of days,
like for hundreds of years
        that the earth fell
        in
        on
        miners
trapping them underground with nothing
but their prayers

This time on April 5th 2010
29 men died
in what they call a "mine disaster"
others, "industrial homicide"
        homicide
        homicide.

DEAD, 29 MINERS
Whatchu know about black diamonds…

You See, When Mrs. Lynch
when sweet Mrs Genny Lynch
heard the news
that her husband would not be coming home
she knew that there would be no more
        "I love you's"
no more three kisses at 4am
no more "coffee on the stove by your bucket, Honey"
Her high school sweetheart

her husband of 34 years
her Rosie,
       would not
       be coming
       home.

When sweet Genny sheds a tear
when every coal wife
sheds a tear
there comes the pressure
       compacted
       compacted
       compacted
and every time Mrs. Lynch, Mrs. sweet Genny cries
and her tears hit the earth
       There
       There
in the mountains of West Virginia, forms a priceless
black diamond
no coal company can ever sell.

These jewels of Appalachia
women who love their men deep into the earth
this special breed
this diamond
forming diamonds
compacted
compacted
       of tears
       of love
       of human slavery
       of the company store

of "we're sorry for your lost"
of black black lung

this/ our history, is scattered
you have to find it in poems
called Black Diamonds
in pages where black ink fades
until somebody digs
and some brave heart will heart will always hear the call
from deep inside the earth and dig
so that millions and millions of years from now...
they will hold up and marvel at our diamonds,
wonder at their timeless love
formed by pressure
     and pressure
     and pressure
and the salt
     of her tears.

JEREMY PADEN

the hills we grew on

when the hills we grew on
disappeared, our parents said:

set down roots near still waters
be grounded. hold on tight

my brother, desperate, consumed
what fauna made him home
until nothing came to roost

my sister sent her tap root deep
busted through limestone & quartz
to reach springs hidden below bedrock

I dreamed the sky is ground & ground sky
sent my roots into the atmosphere

Limb

On Whiteness

In the late 70s, back when perms weren't a fashion statement but simply the way hair was worn, we lived in Rome, Georgia. Mom, who had naturally wavy hair, kept hers, as I remember it, in rather tight curls.

A few years ago we were talking about passing and she told me that once her hairdresser in Rome had asked her, *You sure you're not black. Your olive skin. Your dark, almost black, eyes. Your black curly hair.*

Mom says she laughed and said, *No, honey! My mother's Puerto Rican.*

This story was told about six or seven years ago. Even though it isn't about mom's childhood, the perm story fits a pattern of stories about race and skin color that mom, every once in a while, tells her growing up years. Out of the blue a little biographical anecdote, not connected to any other larger narrative, is shared. Little fragments of surprise and revelation that wash up on the shore and are offered up as curiosities and little more.

Though she grew up speaking no Spanish, mom's Puerto Rican. We've all always known this. My grandfather, a G.I. from central Texas, met and married my grandmother while stationed in Ponce, Puerto Rico. And mom, though raised in north Texas, was born in Aguadilla.

But little stories tumble out. Like the one she shared many, many years ago about how our grandmother wouldn't let her and her brother play outside in the summer. Their skin browned too quickly in the bright Texas sun. And with their jet black hair and their dark eyes, *abuelita*, mom says, feared they'd be taken for Mexican.

I've carried this little tidbit of intra-Hispanic, immigrant dislike around for a long time. And principally understood it as an expression of rivalry between immigrant groups. Yes, a story that shows my grandmother to be both classist and racists and that also points to her fears of not fitting in. A story that goes hand in glove with her refusal to speak Spanish to her children.

But just a few days ago another story came to light. Mom told me that once when visiting the island as a teenager her mother was quite happy when a boy at the pool in Ponce called mom *leche*, for her white skin. It was proof that her regimen of sun abstinence was working. And even more. The catcall *leche*, for *abuelita*, mom said was a vast improvement to the pet name *abuela's* family used for her when she was a child, *negra*.

When I was 12 we moved to the Dominican Republic, and once in the Caribbean began visiting our Puerto Rican cousins quite frequently. Several years into our Dominican residency we learned that *abuela*, Boricua to the core, wasn't born in Ponce, like we'd always thought. Instead, she was born on the neighboring island, our island, the Dominican Republic. That she was born in San Pedro de Macorís, like George Bell, Pedro Guerrero, Sammy Sosa.

This Dominican birth shocked mom. Not because things like birthplace mean much to her, but because origin meant so much to *abuela*. *Abuela* was *Ponceña*—from *La Perla del Sur*, from Ponce, the most genteel city of Puerto Rico. Her family the Mauras, despite the Afro-Puerto-Rican half-brother her *papi* gave the family with that *mujer de la esquina*, were *gente decente*. Founders of universities, of Río Piedras, no less. Most importantly, they were recent immigrants from Spain—not *mezclaos* like the rest of the island. The Mauras were *pura cepa*. Backbone of Ponce. And yet, *abuela* was born on the larger—blacker—island to the west. And she never said *ni pío* about it. Never until she needed her birth certificate.

Abuela's Borinquen pride notwithstanding, her birth on some other island is not surprising. Archipelago people are a people on the move, a people who hop about *por buscarse la suya*. And her *papi* was a man of *negocios* who hoped he could deal a wheel with Trujillo. Until, that is, Trujillo found a reason to want her *papi's* business—or so the story goes—and the family had to sneak back over and live out *papi's* last days like bourgeois fallen on hard times.

Abuela's silence isn't surprising either. In fact, silence, especially biographical silence, is something *abuela* cultivated. She went by her second name, the much less common, Hortensia, instead of Lucía, because she didn't want to be confused with the other Lucía—

Ponce's crazy woman. She spoke no Spanish to her children, spoke only in whispers of her half-brother, kept her Dominican birth quiet.

And we were raised in this silence. I mean, we called her *Ita*. Short for *abuelita*. Knew she spoke Spanish when she'd visit. Knew, even, she was Puerto Rican. But that never meant anything. Not until I was 15 and needed a new passport.

The renewal documents came with census information. And dad asked me, *do you want to be White, Native American, or Hispanic?*

Confused, I said, *but, dad, we're White.*

At that point he told me story of the Padens moving west and of how our name can be found on the Cherokee Rolls. And he also asked, *why do you think you call your mother's mother Ita and not grandma?*

Only then did it really sink in that she was Hispanic. And that this was different than White. It's not that it was a secret. It was just something the family didn't talk about. Plus, most of our growing up years were spent outside the US. And, in Latin America we were *gringos*. We spoke English at home. Celebrated Thanksgiving with other expats. What choice was there but to be White?

And for Ita, she was *Maura*, and *Los Mauras* were Spanish, so recently from Spain, when it came to questions of race they could hardly be Puerto Rican, my grandmother would swear at times.

Whether or not the purity of our Spanish heritage is true, I don't know. I don't know when our Maura's arrived in Puerto Rico. But I also know a certain class of island people insists, even against the mountain of contradictory evidence, that they're nothing but Spanish. But we're recent immigrants, we say. And Maura is a rare surname. So that's something. But, I'm rather sure my grandmother never knew that Maura means Moor, as in from Maghreb, from Mauretania, from Barbary Coast.

This, this forgetting, this covering over in silence all those bits of biography that might not fit the story in its purest sense, this is one of the first moves of whiteness in America.

Of Jíbaros and Hillbillies

for Minnie Curtis y Castor Rivera

The people of the forest speak with a natural wisdom.
Though thousands of miles apart, they find understanding
in the healing powers of Yerbas Buenas.

Call them Curanderos, Jíbaros and Hillbillies.
Birthed in the land and raised by mountains,
they know what it means to live overshadowed
in a place where so many green things grow.

Scotch-Irish, African-Andalucian and Cherokee-Taíno blood
forged them into poets, composers, and great storytellers.
They delight in the flavor of chocolate gravy,
pimento cheese, and the warmth of fresh cow's milk.

From the method of seasoning a black iron skillet
to the baroque manner in which a man courts a woman,
la pobreza de ser campesino no es lo que nos une
si no, la dignida de una vida sencilla.

Rooted

for sister forebears

I like carved out paths,
nicely moved runways,
the salute of oaks bowing,
pussy willows applauding my sway.

I don't mind sauntering behind
the way prepared
and I think Harriet understands,
she and Sojourner shaking
the heads of wildflowers at me
catcalling, *"Go on, Girl!"*
as I step onto their well worn footprints.
It's their hands that press forward
my back, rooted.
Rooting!

"Didn't I knock over trees for you, Girl?"
Ida B. huffs at my spine,
as together they shape smooth
the worry in my brow.
I hang onto them,
who set my skull with grandmotherly palms,
kneading to focus my mind
before the world hardens it.

This is no pampering
as I teeter in the archway,
peek out at miles
where I must add my own step.
No, this laying on of hands
wills instructions.
Mary Bethune solidly lifting my chin,
"Didn't you read mine?"
She straightens my shoulders.
Fannie Lou works her battered limbs,
using them as my divining rod.

This ain't no civil rite.
These women were angry
At my settled softness—
long since they overcame
and I arrived—
chosen by these sisters to model
my own stuff.
Miss Daisy thrusts me her ticket,
bating me sharply,
We bought you that ticket, Girl!"

And they pushed.

Raised by Women

I was raised by
Chitterling eating
Vegetarian cooking
Cornbread so good you want to lay
down and die baking
"Go on baby, get yo'self a plate"
Kind of Women.

Some thick haired
Angela Davis afro styling
"Girl, lay back
and let me scratch yo head"
Sorta Women.

Some big legged
High yellow, mocha brown
Hip shaking
Miniskirt wearing
Hip huggers hugging
Daring debutantes
Groovin
"I know I look good"
Type of Women.

Some tea sipping
White glove wearing
Got married too soon
Divorced
in just the nick of time
"Better say yes ma'am to me"
Type of sisters.

Some fingerpopping
Boogaloo dancing
Say it loud
I'm black and I'm proud
James Brown listening
"Go on girl shake that thing"
Kind of Sisters.

Some face slapping
Hands on hips
"Don't mess with me,
Pack your bags and
get the hell out of my house"
Sorta women

Some PhD toting
Poetry writing
Portrait painting
"I'll see you in court"
World traveling
Stand back, I'm creating
Type of queens
I was raised by women

The Negro Travelers' Green Book: 1957

Mama born this year
       something green come from heaven
say all the folks who say Amen
       There are many legends the old people will recall to you
Baby born black and Green Book says
       Assured protection for the Negro Traveler
mama travels this year
       through the negro traveler
Now we are passing the savings on to you
       the womb is a road bruised black and red
The tense world affairs still smolder
       and our Green Book says
To see and learn how people live
       My mama sees, her mama learns
The White traveler has no difficulty
       Black and read and difficult
Seven children born black
       Until the fear of war eases, we trust you will use your discretion
seven is heaven's number, six is the Devil's
       and mama is the last
knot in the rope, knot of the tree
       green and black, and read, gift of God's
People   an opportunity

Portrait of Mother's Kitchen

Kettle the color
             of Augusta tadpoles
marred by chicken grease and unkept steam
black handle
      worn smooth

Hotcomb resting
             on the leftback burner
stove eye red   glaring
remnants of scalp and ears charred
      between metal teeth

Dead mouse
             in the corner
right side of its head stuck
to a square glue trap
      tail tucked under hind legs
          pupils bulging glossy blind

Spider plant
             in the square window
creeping toward Dollar Store curtains

pressed thin
      gleaming
            floor lit with the smell of pine

Ace of Spades: September 15, 1973

An aging clapboard house leans against the corner of 8th Avenue simulating a low note suspended in the curve of a saxophone. The house is viridian and most of the exterior paint is chipped, withering to the sundial of time. The infrastructure sags in the middle, heavy with the burden of a trumpeted blues, a blues lived by a certain kind of folk in this town. The kind of blues played with a metal slide—wailing in a whiskey still voice on long summer nights behind the backdrop of a jaundiced moon. Sometimes the only relief is a rigid shot of Kentucky Tavern or the snapback of a can of Budweiser or Schlitz. Ten years ago the cornerstone of this American way of life was rocked to the foundation by a dynamite blast from the basement of Sixteenth Street Baptist Church. Only eight blocks from the point of detonation, this structure has witness serious interactions concerning race. The people who frequent this shot house are scarred from years of having to explain, defend, and get along. They live in a city that has been trying to heal the lacerated wound of indifference. The city is still divided on the inside, and on the outside, people get along for the sake of trying—trying to reconcile, get over, and move on. Something easier said than done. And here, in the bootleg house of Pearl Lee, who inherited the house from her mother and mother's mother, resides a communal institution, a meeting place to unwind, relax and have a good time. Here, in Birmingham, a bootleg house can be a person's best friend.

Earlier today, the Jukebox Man drove up in his spanking brand new 73 Bonneville to load Pear Lee's jukebox with black vinyl—.45 discs. In many ways, even though the jukebox man is an interloper in this community, meaning he ain't black—he determines the rhythm of their blues or the octave of voices in card games by the records he selects for the machine. Like tonight, Catbird, with his string bean frame drooping over the glass casing, slips a quarter through the slot and selects a double play of Gene Chandler and Johnny Taylor. He then two-steps with an imaginary dance partner, right hand around the imaginary waist, the left elbow slightly raised, almost pantomiming—and he turns and dips until he floats into the kitchen.

"Hey Pearl, you betta' call the am-bu-lance cause we bout to kill something up in here tonight. Watch out now!" Pearl Lee cannot hear Catbird, as she is up front the big-room. Although Catbird does not work a legal job or cut-a-slave, he stays dressed sharper than a hatchet after the grindstone: Florsheims with silk socks, two-piece dark seersucker suits, and a Dobbs forever tilted on the back of his forehead. Catbird is a numbers runner by trade; he simply refuses to work for Mr. Charlie, thinks a job ain't nothing but another form of owning.

"Catbird sit yo ol'wrinkle ass down. We got one more hand to go and you wanna get up and play some goddamn *running to the end of the rainbow type shit*. Hell, we bout to have yo ass at the end of a rainbow in about five minutes." The voice comes from Sledge, who thinks to herself what the hell Catbird knows about some damn blues. Shit, she lived the blues everyday of the week she woke up and dragged her tired ass down to Deluxe Beauty Shop by 8:30am, a shop she did not own, and by the time she paid the chair fee, all she could do was take care of her rent and come down to Pearl's for whiskey and a laugh.

For Sledge, the thing about digging fingers into a wooly head for a perm or a curl, was not so much the act itself, but what came with the act. She heard more *my man done left me*, or *the rent due and I ain't got two nickels to rub together* problems than she wanted to hear. When a woman sat in her chair, this is what Sledge received: an offering of slow strummed realities fretted from hard living.

"Catbird I ain't playing with yo toothpick looking ass. Why every time we play cards on Friday you gotta act a natural fool?"

"Sledge why I gotta be acting? All I'm trying to do is have a good time suga. Can't a man enjoy himself every now and then?"

"Man you been enjoying yourself since you popped out yo mama womb. Before you step them Florsheims in hell you probably gone ask Lucifer if he got a dollar for shot of red." Defeated in his defense, Catbird sits down. Still, he manages to let out a "you damn right."

There are two other people at the table, Bookie, who is Catbird's partner and Dot, who is Sledge's partner. Before Dot begins her deal, the familiar slide of bedroom slippers gliding across a pale blue linoleum floor signals the arrival of Pearl Lee from up front. Pearl Lee is a rather large, big boned woman, with a steel gray afro and piercing tar-liquid eyes. She enters the kitchen and begins a verbal assault on the man who shacks up with her every night, because a woman in her line of work needs a man around for the physical stuff.

"Bookie how in the hell you gon' pour shots and play cards at the same time?" Paperboy say he wanna pint of gin and two beers brought to the back room where him and that gal Florene at. Man, seem to me, the older you get, the dumber yo black ass get."

Bookie could be called dumb, but that might do him too much justice. He left the corn and cotton fields of Boulder Gee, Alabama back in '40, with only a third grade education to draw words from. The only thing Bookie can do well is work a manual labor job, the one trait he inherited from his daddy. Hard work it was to rise after the moon disappeared into the crevice of night and before the solitary break of sunlight swept across the red clay roads that led to the field. When Bookie turned twenty, he left for Birmingham, stayed for a while right near downtown in Tuxedo Junction, drinking and jazzing with the hipsters. Time has not been good to Bookie. An old man now, he still works hard but has moved no further along in life.

"Now hold on Pearl Lee, you know I'm keepin' an eye on thangs. If a rat move, I know what hole he went into. I on't know why you be all on my back bout lil stuff. I'm gon' take care of ya baby. One hand to go and Dot dealin' right now. Shit, if we win, me and Catbird got a fifth of that good red comin'."

"Fool, I don't care nothing bout no liquor! In case yo dumb ass don't know, I run a damn shot house. And yo ass drinking for free." No one at the table says a word. Pearl Lee means business when she starts cussing.

"Don't worry Pearl Lee, his behind be up in a minute," Dot says while picking up her pile of cards she'd just dealt herself, arranging them in like order with a Kool Filter King dangling off the edge of her lips, the slow glow of red burning brighter when she inhale— the soft ashes at the end hanging on for dear life. She is Pearl Lee's best friend, has the upper advantage when it comes to any kind of sentimentality or compassion concerning Pearl Lee.

"Damn it, I'll do it myself," Pearl Lee goes inside the kitchen pantry, pouring the half pint and grabbing two beers from the Frigidaire. She leaves as she came, sliding her slippers across the floor.

Dot is the wild card within this bunch sitting at the table. The first time she came to Pearl Lee's B.B. King's *Down Home Blues* was jumping out the jukebox on a Friday night.

Her husband Gene brought her so she could see where he came every payday for the past five years. The entire house welcomed her with good music and good drink. Dot is educated with a college degree from Alabama A&M and has a good teaching job in the school system. This kind of life used to be foreign to her; she always thought she was too sophisticated to hang with these folk. But when it came down to it, she realized she was just as down home as the rest of them; had experienced the same kind of blues, the same joys. Pearl Lee took to Dot so much that they were almost like sisters. She was around the place so much now that her husband stopped coming around.

Card games at Pearl Lee's involve a lot of overhand card smacking and shit talking. These are the most serious engagements one can walk into. The rivalry is furious between partners and oftentimes battles take place along gender lines. This one playing out right now is down to the last hand: first one to seven books wins the game of Whist. For the winner there is a bottle of state store whiskey at stake. But there is something else going on in the shotgun house directly behind Pearl Lee's house. The house is rented by Mrs. Two-Bit. Her place is small and doesn't do the business that Pearl Lee does. When Two-Bit's husband Frank retired from US Steel, she decided to make a little extra money by selling liquor to supplement his pension that takes care of them both, plus Two-Bit gets a chance to have company every now and then.

"Two-Bit gimme another shot of whiskey," the man sitting in the kitchen orders.

"Man why you dranking so much tonight? What? You gon' spend the whole paycheck here? Take that money home to your wife and kids." Two-Bit sits in front of the one window in her living room. If she angles her head just right, she can see who comes and goes out of Pearl Lee's house. Two-Bit is also known as the 'Mouth of the South,' and tells everybody's business when she can get her ears and eyes on it.

"Two-Bit why is you worried about my family, woman? I'm spending hard earned money here tonight, that's all you need to know. I spend the money and you pour the dranks, that's how it 'sposed to work." The man's name is Gene. Gene bangs his glass on the table, signaling for Two-Bit to get up and pour another drink.

"Stop making all that damn noise. You know Frank in the back room sleep." Two Bit gets up and lays a half-gallon on the table. "Here's the damn bottle, you gon' pay for the whole thing." Two-Bit returns to the window. She has a small transistor radio tuned to an Atlanta Braves game. She listens and looks between the radio static.

Gene's mind is still on the "noise," a noise that will not stop banging in his drunken head. He had hoped consistent shots of whiskey would evaporate the noise—make it melt away from his consciousness. But it is still there, along with the vision, the one vision a hard working man never wants to see; the kind of images that can twist a man's insides tighter than a tourniquet, a vision that drops the heart heavier than an eight ball in the corner pocket.

Gene couldn't believe what he saw and heard. It was something inconceivable. That day, he just happened to come by Pearl Lee's house during lunchtime from his job down at Acipico Steel. Pearl Lee was not home and when Bookie saw him coming up the back steps, Bookie's eyes bulged a bit and his speech began to stutter.

"Wh…wh—what you do…do—do…doing here this time of day, Gene?"

"Man what the hell wrong with you. You done forgot how to talk now? Gimme a drank. Mr. Charlie down at the mill been riding my back all week bout putting out more work. Man they act like I'm a machine or something. I took lunch early today, my nerves shot man. There gotta be a better to get bill money."

When Gene passed Bookie and sat down by the jukebox, he saw something familiar on the table: a set of keys with a plastic baseball on the ring. The lettering on the ball itself read: Barons. The same kind of key chained he bought his wife at a minor league baseball game last year. Gene picked the keys up and looked at Bookie. Bookie looked like he was about to run a stream of piss down his overalls. The harder Gene looked at him. The harder Bookie sweated.

"Now…now—now… hold on G…G—Gene, it ain't what you think going on here. Sh..sh..sh—she left them keys here this morning before she took Pearl Lee down to the courthouse to pay them fines the police come in and give her the other night."

Gene got up and went in the middle bedroom, grabbed a chair and propped it next to the wall where he and Bookie would sometimes watch people who came in to rent rooms for sex. Gene would then go home and make love to his wife. Bookie stood in the frame of the door, unable to get a word out as Gene stepped up on the chair and placed his eyeball on the small hole in wall that had been carved with a pocketknife.

On the other side of the peephole, lying on the bed with the body of man on top of her was Dot, his wife, the mother of his children; the woman he brought his paycheck home to every week. Her legs said eleven and two, and the man in the middle, was loving her like freight train. Gene saw the orgasmic look on her face as his wife's body trembled until she convulsed uncontrollably. Gene turned from the peephole—an anvil formed in his throat; he could not swallow his own saliva no matter how hard he tried. And when he tried to catch his breath, the voice of his wife echoed through the keyhole once more, driving the stake of betrayal further into his heart, and all he could feel were the strings of Leadbelly plucking in his veins. He looked at Bookie with wet eyelids and ran from the bedroom, crashed through the backdoor—the screen door swinging in the wind. That was the last time Bookie saw him. Bookie never said a word to nobody, not even Dot. Gene never said a word to Dot.

Sitting at Two-Bit's table right now, with the burn of whiskey in his throat, these are the sounds that hunt Gene. He has never confronted Dot about that day, about her infidelity. He has been living with this knothole for almost a year. The last drop of liquor leaves the shot glass and into his throat. His tongue smacks his palate. He digs in his pockets and leaves a fifty-dollar bill on the table.

"Two-Bit I'm gone. I'll see you." Two-Bit gets up and takes the money off the table, realizes it is a fifty. She goes back to her window with the bill in her hand and looks at the silhouette of Gene through screen.

Inside Pearl Lee's, the game is down to the last play of cards. The men and women both have the same amount of books made: six. The next made book determines the winner and will bring the smoothness of Johnny Walker Red and the right to talk shit for a week until the next card game. Everyone at the table is tense. There are a few onlookers in the kitchen, as the game has gotten serious. Even Pearl Lee has left her bedroom up front for a minute to see how this last hand goes down.

"Come on man it's your play." Dot is speaking directly to Catbird. At this point, there is no bluffing or whimsical deceit. One card will either win or lose. Catbird rubs the tattered grey stubble on his chin and slaps his lead-off card on the thin kitchen table. The card spins north by east, revealing the 10 of hearts. He then yells, "teach me how to swim, I can drown with the best of 'em!"

"You gotta brang ass to get ass you old muthafucka!" says Sledge with a flick—release of a defiant jack. Bookie then draws from his third grade education—throws out a trump card—the six of spades, without eye contact.

Bookie yells, "That's right you hair grease smelling heifer! I drank Johnny Walker Red. Sledge don't worry, you can keep that ass—that wrinkled thang be safe with me baby!"

Before the riff of laughter envelops the kitchen, Dot slaps the last card on her forehead. She rotates her neck 90 degrees for Bookie and Catbird to view.

"How bout both of you old crusty muthafuckas kiss my natural black ass, Next!" Glued to Dot's forehead is the ace of spades. There is the beginning of a smile. But this formation of a smile is immediately replaced. The moment her cheeks begin to part, the tracery of a bullet discarded from a .38 special pierces through the black miniature spade on her forehead and bursts her brain into a sea of blackness, she enters that void of the unknown, the uncertainty, but Gene hopes that it is hell. He hopes his wife rots in hell.

"Holy shit!" Catbird says, watching blood seep through the hole in Dot's head. Dot slumps over and her face smacks the table harder than any card played tonight. In the doorway of the kitchen, the raised right arm of Gene is pointed in Dot's direction, smoke from the barrel rising toward the ceiling. He has parted the onlookers deeper than Moses did the Red Sea. The only one who did not flinch or run out the room up is Pearl Lee. She eases her hand on top of Gene's arm and presses the gun barrel downward. Bookie, Sledge and Catbird are still at the table, watching the blood as it begins to coagulate on the table. Pearl Lee looks at Bookie. The next play on the jukebox is B.B. King's *The Thrill is Gone.*

the good couch

in the living room
sat the couch
an oatmeal tweed burlap thing
one of them splurge items
purchased spontaneously at value city
and for the good couch reason
my parents covered it with a sheet of plastic
a foggy, heavy, synthetic skin
that rustled with every motion
as we sat all those years
attached to the couch
and bound to the only television
when summers smothered up
scorching hot days
back when home AC
was a myth to me
something not felt but alluded to on TV
on those simmering evenings
primetime bubbled across
blue flickering screens
the family filed onto the couch
filling it to capacity
and the windows left open
with upright fans propped
circulated stale humid breezes

our convection oven house
broils us on couch spits
its transparent epidermis
hungering for exposed flesh
nipping at legs and arms
wrapping
biting and suffocating
and of course
i would have to wait
until the next commercial break
because the sound of me ripping
clean from the velcro couch
would've drowned out the TV
and everyone would have thrown a fit
'cause cosby
might have said something witty
full sweater
in his air-conditioned brownstone

learning how to use motherfucker

a boy named Man must be your first best friend
made in a project, so your momma says.
he once grinned as he choked-out his pet Doberman
with a fat gauged chain,
giggled thunder as he rained warm piss
on your face from the tree tops,
smirked and chomped into your sister's forehead
like a gold'n'delicious
leaving a tooth-punctured "C"
you'd wish he'd just stopped coming by
like you wished daddy just stopped coming home
but assumed neighbors we're just like family
so you mimicked Man to avoid his wrath

that day, like Man, you kneeled limestone
an anxious parrot on his shoulder
skipping crushed Colt 45 cans across the street
like creek slate at the big kids along with names
that five-year-olds call big kids in an octave
too low for the big kids to register.
frustrated, Man's face got real still
then he launched a word like a mortar
of four rhythmic syllables
that's echoed and dive-bombed every ear
drum within earshot from grown folks

perched on porches to the teens
straddled along fences flirting
smiles and laughs crept across their faces
as they murmured about what
 "little badass Man" had said
and you wanted some of that action
some of that that attention
so you tapped into that primordial word
that you knew deep in your bones
and sent it out spinning into the world
like unleavened hot aluminum
and watched as
everyone
as everything
stopped
and time
dilated

you watched from the outside
as the multigenerational mob led by Man
rabidly, joyously chanting "Aww,
(insert name here)
said M-F-er, your daddy's gonna beat you"
as they dragged your body, your paled
and frightened face home,
you wailed as your naked butt was lashed
for five minutes on the porch
for a live audience but all you could do was glare
at Man's dirty face through a wet veil
as he hysterically pointed
knowing and saying over and over again
in your head only

that you would never speak to that
motherfucker ever again

Burying Albatross

In the parking lot behind the funeral home, my eyes settle on
the bulky white noose my father has lost a wrestling match to.
Though he is not convinced Windsor knot know-how can plant
tobacco or drive a nail true, he concedes his flawed results,

abides my desire to fix it. Calling up knowledge passed to me
from a book, I execute the maneuvers with fluid precision
and imagine I am creasing and folding a Japanese paper swan.
He stares at my knuckles, smiling, perhaps seeing his own hands

stuccoing a high ceiling or replacing a worn out alternator.
Standing close enough to kiss, we almost touch and pretend
to bury other heavy things, sewn together like the opposite ends
of the fabric in my hands. Before I let him go, all the sage advice

and words of encouragement that never breathed air between us
spread a silent wing then slide through a perfect slip knot, home.

ELLEN HAGAN

American Arabic, Irish, Italian Abecedarian w/ Blue(d)grass & Bourbon(d) Influences

Alphabetize existence: adage, acreage, age: under, old, less (is more—or is it?)
behold bourbon barrel B-town baby (girl), believer in bats, bells & boom boxes
causing cold chills in chlorine contaminated city pools
dreaming days of dodging disasters
existing to elevate—elevation &
fetch, fast forward float.

Gargantuan(ly) gussied up, no guise, all gall gall, gall, all gumption & good
hell of a hellion—high water(ed), heathen(ed) hexer of helium & high(ed) hopes
inclusion in instrumental, illustrious illusions, inventions
justifying the jut & juke & jaw of juvenile—cause I was
king of kin & kegs, kites the kind you could keep
like lightning, like lithium, like lunacy, lunatic (like).

My mom & my mom's mom, & my mom's mom's mom & more, more
never enough, all the time too much, too much, too much
or, otherwise known as ointment, orbiting orchard or outlaw, outdo, overdone
perhaps punk rock pixie girl of pulp & plumes
quite often confused for quirk & wit quick, never quaint or (un) questioned
right up to righteous & rowdy & raucous, rambunctious & rank
straight salient, (in) (un) satiable, same, sane & (in) sane.

True, tall tales of trouble trailed me always
utterly, undone & untied (tidy), understand the urgency of un-rooted, unraveled
verify, let me verify the vulnerabilities—they are vast & vain
why don't you witness—wait watch the way these worries get
xeroxed & xeroxed, X marks every
yearning
zon (ed) zenith

Even Tricksters Get the Blues

I have been sick all day and finally my body and house
are quiet. Is not *quintessential* a word that hides quills
to avoid questions? Saw a slow show about Whitman's
vexed aging, read Ritsos' last bitter poems about wondered

if Anna Akhmatova was forced to use her fire poems
as kindling in her last years? How quixotic I thought
Death was after I read the Romantics—before AIDS,
war(s), my friends stolen in broad midnight. Better

that I eat this banana bread my lover made or think
about not thinking, but not like in Buddhism. I do not
think this world is an illusion; I have eaten mangos,
have been transparent in a sudden cloudburst, and have

watched the doctors strap me down so I would not
loosen tubes by movement. I have been moved by bad
radio, fucked in a foreigner's taxi, danced on a rooftop
Sunday mornings while other below filed toward

a staid God. But nothing is enough. And Dylan, rage,
is not exactly a Plan A. My black stray cat is in her
perch, very *Moby Dick* (hey, scholars the copyright
is dead in the waters). More and more, I am dreaming

in the Spanish of my skeptical childhood—does this
mean I am healing, or not? Am I flying backwards to
the blackness before birth or am I trusting the Santería
women who hissed, *so sad by you will have a long*

life? I was 18 and expected a long penis. My religion
has always been based on how the body is ground zero.
My Native friends pray for me even though I am Columbus'
heir. They say, *funny how doctors cannot find our souls.*

I work hard to forgive all gods for not being in my image.
When I feel weak, I smell oranges, as if my mind is lost
in an orange orchard. A warning? A path home? Oranges
wait to be naked as I peel them with my trembling hands.

PANTONE 130 C

He'd never seen a creole girl with freckles before. Everyone he knew was molasses: smooth as crawdads steamed in paper sacks, pot roast Sundays—slow, just as tender. But she was more how bees make honey: furious, purposeful. Even if the end result was slow the work was sugar—productive, mindlessly soft. She chews octaves into the barrels of Ticonderoga #2's as he sat behind her in their school desks. Now & then, the plastic of her chair would catch the curled tips of the braids her mama plaited for her. He'd swat loose the coils like tree from hive. Much he wanted to cut them loose with a pair of paper scissors, catch the loose wisps in a jar where he knew they would punch against the glass like lightning bugs. The ceiling fan billowed the nape of her hand-me-down pinafore, her undershirt, the scent of lemon pound cake underneath. Chalk scrawls on the blackboard as she absently dreams of Algebra. The paint flecks of pencil like a school bus embarking the dimples of her lips.

DANNI QUINTOS

Pond's White Beauty

My sister & I watch a commercial:
twin Filipina beauties washing their faces.

They splash water like diamonds, velvety
suds. Black silk hair & smooth, pink apple

cheeks, both paler than any relatives
we've met here, paler than the quiet Welsh

& Japanese blood in both of us. On the screen
a blind date in a blazer rings the doorbell.

The more porcelain sister answers—
her fluorescence lights his stupid smile.

The door opens wider to reveal her
apricot twin: flushed with melanin

next to the sharp, pallid sister. The man frowns.
We frown, knowing that the next scene

will be the sister sharing her secret
potion: Just use Pond's White Beauty

fairness cream to bleach the sun from your
skin, to make you milky translucent.

The second date he sees them both
glowing ghostly identical, laughing

at how beautiful they've both become,
unable to tell which girl is his date.

We are two sisters in the middle
of the world where the sun paints us

bronze. In the dark instant between
commercials, our brown faces appear

in the TV's glass, where their blanched
& smiling ovals once shone.

Portrait of My Dad Through a Tent Window

Ramirez was on the loose. First name Angel & the news made him a monster. A cop in my driveway asking Dad if he'd seen this man, but maybe switching his glance back & forth from the photo to make sure my brown dad with long hair wasn't him. Before we knew about this train-hopping killer, Dad bought us a tent with two rooms & set it up in the backyard. Shelli & I cracked Sprite cans open & Dad washed dark red cherries & put them in a bowl for us. Our flashlights made hand shadows into geese & talking dogs, made our ghost story faces monstrous, light shining up our noses. We kept the tent's window unzipped, a grey screen crawling with coppery beetles. While the train's howl lulled us asleep, we could see just beyond their bodies: Dad in the yellow-lit kitchen window, watching the lights jump around the tent.

Nightstick

in Kentucky you are a Black girl, but don't know. you sleep
next to it. crooked bone, split-open head. patrolling through the night.
don't even know you should be trying to run away. it rests
in your night terrors, in a bureau between your grandmother's quilts,
with her thimbles & thread & dead white poems. don't think
for a moment your grandfather won't pull it out, make a cross of it
with your arms, gift you its weight & crime. do you believe?
what if he said its name was *Justice*? would that be too much?
if he was the only man your childhood saw hauled away in handcuffs,
pale & liver-spotted & stiff in limbs sharp enough to fold into the back
of a cruiser? you. this bruise of irony. the only two Blacks ever allowed
in his house. & at night he be singing you to sleep while it sits invisible,
sentry-like out of sight. he be humming hymns—*i come to the garden alone*
while the dew is still on the roses—knowing how much blood it has seen &
whose. he be holding you to himself like a secret & every song be a prayer
for your daddy's sunk-in head. you breathing one for his whole face
before you. bullying a shit-shaded boy's head is what it's made for,
he say, your papaw, while you hold it, not knowing enough about yourself
to understand the cannibal nature of chewing on his words with no riot
inside. no baton twirling in the air of your stomach. no notice of the grand
wizard & his wand when he appears in your nightmare. you be closed-eye
& it be there, Black as who it means to beat

The Dark Room

After Carrie Mae Weems's "You Became a Scientific Profile/ An Anthropological Debate/ A Negroid Type/ & A Photographic Subject."

You tintype
You daguerreotype
You ambrotype
You cataloged proof of what can be developed
what can be dodged & burned
immersed & fixed in dark rooms

Forward facing you are a question posed
Side profile you are the predicated subject
teaching the difference between taking
and making a picture.
I gaze,
fully aware of whose framing hand,
whose sandblasted words worn across the chest,
whose blood tinged lens
clicks.

Robotto Mulatto

I am the Robotto Mulatto
the day walker, the glimmer in the night
I am the ambiguous apparition
       shifting colors like a conch shell
I am the Halfrican Hulk
the onerous Oreo who will not let you know
       where these big lips come from

I am more than meets the eye
My skin separates along perfect tan seams
       lifts with a hydraulic hiss
       flips in on itself
       and transforms cultures
my skin is controlled like a remote
       with the styling of my hair
       I shift color circuits
       first mustached Mexican, now bearded Egyptian,
       maybe the mysterious collage of whatever
       your half-cousin is

my words are double edged knives,
I can say things that you can't say
       because I have one foot in your door
       and another go-go gadget foot in someone else's

and when all else fails I have a race card
        up each sleeve.

My life is a tug of war between
        being fully Clark Kent and Superman
I don't understand the master/slave jumpers
        on my hard drive
can't fully hug or hate my white motherboard
my weakness is that silicon valley
        isn't big enough for the idea of me,
        and that around here things move so fast
        that before the world is ready for me
        I'll have already become obsolete

Tongue

Social Justice Prayer

On this day, at this moment with this breath.
En este dia, en este momento, con este respiro.

We evoke the communal spirit of justice.
Nosotros evocamos el spirito de comunidad y justicia.

We break bread with our neighbors, we extend our hand to our enemies
and we pray for global justice.
*Nostros partimos el pan con nuestros vecinos, estendemos nuestras manos al enemigo
y pedimos por justicia universal.*

We feed our souls with the courage of those who have dared to
break the silence of oppression.
*Nostros le damos de comer a nuestras almas con el valor de aquellos que tuvieron el coraje de
romper el silencio de la oppression.*

We honor the holy places of protests, the streets, the marches, the public halls,
the seat on the segregated bus, the brown hand who refused to pick the grape,
the power to love in spite of hatred and shame, and we are strengthened by
the conviction of those who dared to spit in the master's soup.
*Nosotros honoramos los lugares santos de protesta, las calles y desfiles,
los pasillos politicos, el asiento en la guagua segregada, la mano mora que no
recogio la uva, el amor que ama envuelto en verguenza y recibimos fuerza
en la convicion de aquellos que escupireron en la sopa del patron.*

On this day, on this moment with this breath.
En este dia, en este momento, y con este respiro.

We promise to bring water and hope to the thirsty immigrant.
Nosotros prometemios traer agua y esperanza al imigrante con sed.

We demand access for the less abled bodied amongst us.
Nostros demandamos acceso a los que el cuerpo no les funcionan bien.

We rejoice in the inherent goodness of all people.
Nosotros regosamos en la inherente bondad de todas las personas.

We worship in all names given to the holy ones and we pray:
Nosotros resamos en todos los nombres de dios y pedimos.

For the marriage of compassion to power.
Por el matrimonio de compasion y poder.

For the abundance of the earth to feed the mouths of hungry.
Por darles de comer a las bocas hambrientas con la abundancia de la tierra.

On this day at this moment with this breath we pray.
En este dia, en este momento con este suspiro rezamos.

We pray that our men and boys claim their true masculinity and bring
their hearts to their genitals.
Resamos por nuestros hombres y ninos, pedimos que ellos reclamen la verdadera masculinidad y
que unan sus corazones con su sexualidad.

We pray that our women and girls grow strong, safe, and free.
Pedimos que nuestras mujeres y ninas crescan seguras, fuertes y libres.

And we pray for us the justice workers, that we may have a circle of family and friends to come home to and for a lover who is willing to wash our aching feet.
Por un circulo de familia y amigos en nuestras casa y por un amante que nos labe nuestros adolorides pies.

Namaste, Amen

ASHA FRENCH

Mama Outsider:
Reminder Notes to a Dancing Girl

The weekend before my white-ish roommate kicks me and my daughter out of her house, she tries to kiss me at a drag show. This, after I told her about my brain. The crippling effects of cortisol. The way I need safety before I can think of any of that other shit. The way even thinking about being romantic with a person with whom I am communal is destabilizing. All the ways you can say "no" without being offensive, without being a Black bitch, without barking like the other dogs she rescues as community service.

It is the weekend Beyoncé releases her "Formation" single and a bad queen has just performed it without breaking a sweat. I am watching the queen and learning that the way not to sweat is to move so little that every move seems like drma. I've got the not moving part down, which is how I am here at a club with a roommate whose friends want to meet the Black girl she let live in her house.

Slightly tipsy, I yell, "Yes!!!" a little too loudly for present company as soon as I hear the first few measures of "Formation." My roommate and her friends laugh, thinking it alcohol and not Black girl magic rising up in me, calling out to my wished-for cousins in the room. I spot one cousin across the way, locs swinging as she and her girls cheer the queen on. Where their hips are free, mine are locked in place between two friendly-enough people I won't get to know. In fifteen minutes, one will destabilize my life with her advances and the other will start crying. I focus on these would-be cousins, wishing to be with them. Wishing to be winding in the company of friends. Wishing for dance ciphers and yelling, "Yes!" and "Get it!" and "Okay!" and "I see you!" and "Do your thang!" and "Werk!"

Dear one, you do not know that you are already dancing. That you are perfecting the dip you learned so long ago. That even when you are low-low, your core holds you up. You will wind slowly until you stand again. Your girls are screaming, "Yes!"

I am fifteen and my friend's mother has thrown her a backyard party. The boys stand on the periphery of our dancing circles because they know where they are. There are mamas and aunties and grandmas and big cousins standing around. This is different than dancing in the absence of adults, in the teen parties where some boys think that winding is an invitation for them to lean their hips in (sometimes with their boys holding them up from behind) while some girl works them into a frenzy. There is no negotiation of sexuality going on at this party, which is one reason the gods send in Big Cousin to teach us another kind of lesson.

Big cousin is probably 19 and she is 1997 Louisville fine, which is a roller wrap, lip gloss with the brown line, and white eyeliner on the eyelids. She is teeshirt tucked in tight jeans fine and she has come through loudly with her girls. I know to take note. I know my life is about to change. I know there is something these young women will teach me about being grown, so I'm taking notes in the socially awkward way of writers that most interpret as staring to the point of disrespect. I've learned to hide the camcorders of my eyes to avoid confrontation so I disappear into the background of the party. And then her song comes on. Cousin drops it low, her butt nearly to the ground, then brings it up slowly, hips rotating to the beat. These are four of the longest measures I've ever heard. The song escapes memory, but Cousin does not. She is laughing at herself when she gets back up, says something like, "Y'all ain't ready," before bouncing off to the next relative, some grown auntie shaking her head and saying "That girl's too much," in a way that is the highest compliment to black girls, in that way that black women learn to mix pride and worry and arrive at hope. Proud that she's "too much." Worried that the world will try to take her down to size, fit her into its tropes no matter what limbs must be cut off to do so. Hope that "too much" will be enough to resist, to wreck that shit.

I am forever changed. This dip becomes my signature move and I will practice it in mirrors until I master it. And I know I have mastered it when I feel my body moving with my memory. The integration, embodiment. I practice and in practicing find freedom to be wild. To be too much. I learn to listen for the code in the base, to hear rhythms telling my hips what to do. I dance wild. I dance freaky. For the next few years, someone taps me on the shoulder to pull me away from the spectacle I am making of myself. Soon, I will be grown enough for nobody to care.

Dear one, it is because you are grown that everyone cares. You destabilize world order with your womb, your winding, your wild ways. Ignore the tapping and take the floor. Find water when you are thirsty then return. Should your dancing bring unwelcome attention, your real girls will fuck somebody up before they try to sit you down. You are fine.

After the drag show it will take a while to remember just how fine I am. Homelessness requires re-memory for all the disses. Displacement, dis-ease, the disaster of living with someone who no longer wants you in their space. It clings to you like grime, like that which makes people avert their eyes. You forget to put on your fine, to perform it until it is real again. And then the gods send Cousin Patricia to your Facebook inbox, Patron Saint of Black Girl Fine. She's the first one who taught you that fine is not the stuff you were born with or even the stuff other people put on you. That stuff is just baggage you root around in until you find your mascara.

"You never put on mascara before?" Patricia asked in shock, bopping her head to the beat of JJ Fad's "Supersonic." I am six and on my first road trip without my nuclear family. I am in route to my godmother's house, a big girl trip, and Patricia's house is a stop along the way. I am six and in awe of teenage girls. The mingling of grown-up and child in bodies are like mile markers pointing me to my "one-day-soon." I put spritzed bangs, popped collars, and mascara on my list of all the ways I will learn how to be fine when I get to be her age.

Patricia also knew how to pick up the needle so as not to scratch the vinyl when she started our song again. By the third repeat, I forgot that I was lonely and I learned to say, "Eenie meenie disaleenie oo wop bop aleenie…" I learned what it means to be something else—a member of this free floating kinship that is humanity and full of cousins you didn't even know you had. It means mascara and the latest dance, Supersonic on repeat and lipsyncing in the mirror. Feeling ourselves, feeling flyy, feeling baaaad and too good to be worried about what they say outside safe doors.

Dear one, be something else. Be Louisville fine and dropping low to bring it up. Be bringing wreck to parties and when they ain't ready, just laugh. Be Supersonic—they cannot steal your voice. Be cousin and connected. Be always holding someone's hand. Sooner than you know, you will be home.

Initiation

for Rachel Eliza

Your friend has entered the tribe
of those who've buried their mothers,
and she is different—more of herself
than ever, but a new layer, the affect
of one unable to shake the sounds
of leaving, to unsee profound rising
preceding her own, waiting. *What day
is it, does it matter? Where am I,
the keys?* Inducted into a society
of hurried truces and anointing
that becomes a steady hum
in the music of all things.

The full, gray sky held its water
as she rained and rained, a rain
that will never dissipate, her legs
forgetting for a spell why they were made,
her husband's arms remembering
what they're for. Shining, gorgeous grief—
death's anchor a terrible salvation to a family
adrift. The sob and tremble of *gone,
gone* coursing through clasped hands.

The duty of firstborn daughters,
how it lengthens the spine and hollows
the cheeks as she holds the widower's hand.
Her crowded face in the mirror,
the morning walk with the "grand-dog"
ambushed with epiphany (oh, the babies
she won't meet!) At any hour, snippets
of speech, sensation and memory surge—
stranding former selves as starfish and conchs
strewn on some remote beach. The thought
of calling, of being called stopped
in its tracks   *No—the ground opened*
and we gave her back,
shut down the interstate and
stood without falling among
all of those stones.

When mothers are lowered, daughters
break out of boxes, unbossed by
the minutia that comes with breathing.
You saw it happen, see it in your friend's
furrowed brow, the revised way she leans
in a doorway, across a kitchen counter.

Her mother has gone there, dragging her
into a new here and her gait has changed.
This missing flares. Gone is the banter
of carefree homegirls; a deeper cadence reigns—
that grown alto, *mama* heavy
on her tongue, loud and loving
in her mind, lucid dreams.
Heiress to her mother's wellspring and might,
she finally gets what *hmph* really means.

When mothers are planted,
daughters begin a furious blooming.

127 Notebooks

for Nikky Finney

Back to your 14th year of living—
eagle eye, iambic breath—
127 spines numbered to the birth
of your recording, textual soundtrack.
I imagine 14-year-old Lynn Carol Finney
is light years more profound
than that number normally allows,
how fallen leaves dance through your pages,
play possum for others. How the carloads of books
your father bought, brought home,
were treasure, your lens growing
ever wider in the listening. Back to the sugar
of South Carolina sun, the way
the day boils & cools, leaves night
for the reckoning: the butterfly
you find dried on your windowsill,
wings as maps, traces of future
to follow. These precious thoughts
wrapped between the covers, held
with both arms to your heart.
The things
you know,
girl. The poem

you will pick from journal #7
in the year of journal #17. The spines,
the spines. Back, back, sweet history,
The oddity & odd number
of 127, never awkward
in the ear's turntable.
How the story
always finds its way.

Answer the Call

"I need you. I need y'all's help. I can't do this by myself"
—Sandra Bland

Can you hear it? A faint whisper at first
trickling in from the ether. A cool hush
against your heart. Be still. Listen
to the words flicker,   *I need you.*   You,
not some other doer busy with the living.
You, of heart and spirit, can you hear
Sandy speak? It's louder now, burrowing
through your spine. Can you feel it
pull you to your feet, feet to pavement
from Illinois to New York, from Waller County
to Austin, Texas? This work, this woman.
You've seen her in the market, on the street.
She is your sister, your friend, your reflection
pinned against the mirror. A crack across
the glass meant for you to swallow. Spit
back. Answer the call. Say her name.
Carry it forward into a new world.

STEPHANIE PRUITT

A Study in Sound and Silence

after "Rehearsal" by John Bankston

Sometimes I mouth the words to hymns,
No sound coming from my throat.
Call it lazy?
Call it memory lapse?
Call it a simple show?   No.

Call it faith in the voice of the audience,
A belief in an other's
Ability to fill in the blanks.
Call it rehearsal:
Visualizing the path in advance of my steps.
Showing up
Despite my moments of disbelief,
Hanging the whole picture of me, all complete
And in progress

We Were Being Detained

before the thirty-six of us could bless the food, he called us out of the names
we resist leaving. quick to accuse, the room of rearranging, to kill him

when no one begged his fall. an impulse born in him, to drag us flat across
a floor we weren't on and we embarrass quietly, laugh and throw pillows to save

necks from the corners of coffee tables. all the scared children, their urgent questions
we wish we could unfold for them, rattle us. i wanna vanish from this detainment.

leave only this body in the room, where the all-star pitcher, who "should've made it
to the league," can't control his saliva. none of this melts down before the wads

of stale entertainment. i say to my guest, "let's just go fix our plates together."
too hungry to let him finish! the lips in the room, too cold to be kissing! i wanted

him to stop what he wouldn't stop so bad! i wanted to see the night zipped up
again, to kill what always happens to him, until what happens to him is cut out!

For Drunk Mike

you must have found jefferson davis
in the bottom of the flask you smuggled
into the house rupp built

your great great grandaddy must have
held his branding iron tight in his grave
& gleamed with pride as he watched you hurl
slurred lashes from whiskey lips past rows
of white faces until they landed onto brown
& black bodies awaiting their chance
to be bought & sold

you must have thought me Ralph Ellison's
invisible so as we shared an armrest
I kindly ignored your elbow
rubbing mine while you unscrewed
another sip unleashing your ancestors
so they could watch too

my eyes searched the rafters for comfort
but instead read the names & years
frozen in time dangling above spectators
who know exactly how much
profit all those bodies made for free

I can't help but wonder
what you really mean by

If I was coach cal
I'd whip them boys
into shape

DORIAN HAIRSTON

Manifesto for Black Baseball Players

Persona—Josh Gibson

never forget the 42 reasons
baseball is best played color blind

steal bases like they
stole this country

break into record books
turn more than just they ink black

pretend the ball is named
jim crow

colonize
the hall of fame

remember we gave the game
lights helmets and color

never be controlled
by anything white

belt *Lift Every Voice and Sing*
during they national anthem

find you a Helen drop down on one knee
place a baseball field on her finger

RANE ARROYO

The Piñata Boy

The police ask me again and again:
were you trying to seduce them?
My broken nose turns me into
living Greek statuary. Phillip lets

limber strangers beat him only if
they agree on a magic word for
stop: *camera!* It's not one he'd
used by accident with a skinhead.

Mannequins in leather guard us
in Boystown against adulthood.
Bonnie visits with yet another
black eye for jewelry. She speaks

of true love as if a burden. One
cop leans forward: *these are college
kids. Will you ruin their futures
by pressing charges?* The rally

isn't about anger, as it should be.
These are my streets too. Angel
says he's never been gaybashed,
as if it's my fault for my purpled

face. Todd gives soldiers blowjobs,
if they're in uniform: *the battle front
has always been at home.* Another
cop shakes his head: *why didn't*

you fight back? Because my two
fists weren't enough against them,
because I want world peace. Glenn
writes a theater review: *What if*

Cabaret was updated with neo-Nazis?
My students see I'm human at last.
My face heals as the attackers are
given probation: *boys will be boys.*

Father would wave his belt but
was unable to fix me. I'm not
broken, Papi, and I won't break for
you. The S&M club screamed

when we dragged in two women
for drinks: NYC wasn't ever Sodom.
The police make a press statement:
the victim should have known better.

Than to exit? Manuel, just out of jail,
shows a black tattoo of a fist clenching
a rose. It covers up a knife wound
and makes him handsome, winsome.

Sí, we refuse to become anyone's
martyrs. Maybe the thugs were trying
to seduce me, the piñata boy of their
wet dreams. *See*, says Ann, *no stars*.

I Hate Crowds or Yippy Ki Yay Murica, FUCK YO COUCH!!!!

where is my filter? where is my leforge visor?
that can instantly shield my eyes from THIS this is
how is it that / buy now / that's not factory equipment?
the capacity to filter out the #alllivesmatters
how is it that white folk don't see the insult in telling me
all lives matter? did something somehow imprint upon your own genetic code
that reacts to anything nonwhite with code speak? i understand you
live in a world in which your likeness (to some degree) is the measuring stick
no matter how inaccurate. have you become bored with all of this?
your nose blindness is impressive if not terrifying / narcissism and insecurity IS
quite the cocktail you've sipped from the tit
after slipping from the womb swashbuckling and swinging from umbilical cords
you little cowboy you. probably got one of those 6 shooters with a holster
for a white christmas. bang bang!!!!!!!!!!!!!!! the sheriff says. you have a plastic badge
that has you believing you are a child of destiny
another imperfect form created in that archetype mold. are you
the next believer in manifest destiny?
the next john wilkes booth? fred phelps? joe mccarthy? james holms?
the next john wayne? clint eastwood? joe paul franklin? george zimmerman. you buckaroo
pop those caps child. no longer finger pointing a fake gun. you are well on your way to capping
fell in love with that smell. not quite thermite. but love was still in the air
pop pop pop. Injuns, chinks, niggers. pop pop pop. It doesn't matter who
as long as you ride off into the sunset
while the sun sets forever on the enemies you have

created, deceived, perceived, lynched.
i use to think that affluenza was the most coward defense one could make
the belief that wealth breeds the ignorance to get away with murder.
this is the foundation that is cracked but there. a white man that murders and walks is well
on its way. into becoming a birthright the stand your ground crowd
the lets build a wall crowd
the blue life crowds
the love it or leave it crowd
the i'm protecting my premises crowd
the i'm protecting my family crowds
the i'm protecting America crowd
the go back to where you came from crowd
the my family were real immigrants crowd
the i don't want my taxes to pay for others healthcare crowd
the get a job crowd
the this country is turning into the third world crowd
the white man is oppressed crowd
the i have it made but hate my life crowd
the playing field is level crowd
the racism doesn't exist anymore crowd
the they're all lazy crowd
the if they had more guns this wouldn't have happened crowd
the he's a muslim crowd
the he wasn't even born here crowd
the share law is taking over america crowd
the he founded isis crowd
the who cares if they have clean water to drink crowd
the they should have gotten into their suvs and left new orleans before katrina hit crowd
the blacks kill more whites than whites kill blacks crowd
the fox news parasite crowd
the my ancestors come from europe/not africa crowd
the we need more oil lets take theirs crowd
the we speak english here no matter where here is crowd

the my behavior and attitude is that of a sympathizer of hate crowd
the jesus was white crowd
the i don't see color crowd
the i got a black joke promise you won't get offended crowd
the you can't take a joke crowd
the godchildren of imperialist actions crowd
the thank god that isn't me crowd
the i shop at walmart because i love a deal before i love america crowd
the i will threaten the police with a gun and live to talk and laugh about it crowd
the i hate everything that doesn't look like me unless it is entertaining me crowd
the they shouldn't have been selling lose cigarettes crowd
the they shouldn't have been selling cds crowd
the they don't live in this neighborhood crowd
the they shouldn't have moved into the neighborhood crowd
the they shouldn't have taken the job crowd
the they must have stolen that car crowd
the they shouldn't have been in the car obeying orders crowd
the they shouldn't have been in the park with a toy crowd
the you surprised me with how well you read and write crowd
the they shouldn't have been standing there crowd
the they shouldn't have looked me in the eye crowd
the you don't talk back to me crowd
the i will stand my ground crowd
the he looks suspicious crowd
the look at my new couch crowd
the my 2nd amendment trumps your life crowd
the he shouldn't have been walking back from the store crowd
the i would have shot him too crowd
the i will run you down in the street with my truck crowd
the all lives matter crowd
the lets make america great again crowd
the lets make america white again crowd
and that is why i hate crowds

MITCHELL L.H. DOUGLAS

Is It Wrong

that I ignore the Witness @ my door, turn back
to the kitchen, pour

another cup of coffee, whisper
Mercy?   I know

what you'll say, no different
than the last visit, arms

full of Watchtowers, a Bible, always
in twos—some kind

of safety.
            I can't

            blame you,
but if we aren't talking

about bullets, I don't
want to ponder

salvation. I don't want
to ignore Altons & Philandos

& how
on earth

did they get those marquee names?
Were their mothers

seers, did they know
their sons

would be #s, footnotes? If
I answer the doorbell that cuts

& drums the hollow
of this house, the blood

you raise in conversation
will not be Sandra's or Rekia's

& what's the use, I think. Don't ask
me about a kingdom,

don't ask
if I've been saved.

NORMAN JORDAN

One eyed critics

3:30
In the morning
With not
A soul in sight
We sat
Four-deep at
A traffic light
Talking about how
Dumb and brainwashed
Some of our Brothers and Sisters are
While we waited
For a green light
To tell us
When to go.

Where Do People in Dreams Come From?

Have you ever wondered
Where people in dreams come from
Those colorful sacred busy people
Coming alive every night in our dreams

Sometimes complete strangers
Sometimes people we know
Deceased people
Especially our loved ones

Appearing as children or adults
Capable of instantly changing to someone else
Performing marvelous feats
Walking fastly backwards; flying without wings

Mostly friendly ordinary people
Making you feel wonderfully excited and extravagant
But sometimes mean evil scary people
Chasing you until they trap you in a corner

When you try to scream
No words come out of your mouth
As they reach to grab you
You miraculously escape by waking up

That's why I ask the question
Where do those magical people in dreams come from
And do they continue to exist while we are awake
Waiting for us to fall asleep again?

AMANDA JOHNSTON

Another Morning Blessed Be

Eggs over easy
A man's daily ritual perched
Down the road, a woman
Grinds her teeth on religion
Brown as chewed tobacco
Emptied from a rusty tin cup

bacon and hash with toast
under a dog eared morning
swollen with milk
offered to a southern God
no one misses once used then
left to crack and chip

strong coffee to take the edge off
paper that says no work today
for sons born under the wrong sign
turned ornery and deaf to prayers
poured to the ground
under a vexed summer sky

Augury

> "...*and they were coming toward him*
> *in rough ranks.*
> *In seas. In windsweep. They were*
> *black and loud"*
> —*Gwendolyn Brooks*—*"Riot"*

Soon enough. All day was filled with the floating dead
of clouds. Children,

throwing birds, guns for thumbs
and forefingers.

My heart is a mineshaft of canaries
and shells.

My smell is filled with flying
and what a sky this is.

Lying on my side,
looking where his eyes might be.
The Northern European still lifes
depicted so many flowers.

The dead teach us that kind of patience. Here I am
lying raccoon-like on the ground, the staccato line.

How different the drawings of a people must be
who have always this kind of time.

***

A brief history of rope:
some of us are brown
as starvation.

Happenstance is the color
of our eyes.

***

What happens when you stare into the sun?
A crow is born. From here, I think
about the image of God.

How He set jagged stars
in the square holes of us.

***

And what are groups of us called?
It is an unkindness

of ravens, for instance. For instance,
        a dole (an offering)
of doves.

We've always been more glorious as a flock.
Groups of us are congregations.

What is more godlike than peace (other than insurgence),

than quiet, as of the breathing of evening
birds, the low warble of our people in the trees.

        ***

Sometimes a dream is a fist you grow into,
but more often, a routine, like watering a weed in your stomach.

        ***

We haven't been made afraid of trees. Nor the bottoms of cars.
Windows, the gavel, the sea.

A feather is caught in the rapture of a fence,

keeps struggling—can't come to terms—
cannot unthink that it's a bird.

        ***

What gives the ground the right
to gravity? No building.
I want to widen the eyes
of God. Every amendment has followed through
against our bodies.
Icharus leapt. We will fly,
be black together in the sun.

Black Bone

I've heard tell
it's part mountain root,
part wellspring.

Others say it's dark matter
threaded through stars, hidden
even from the telescopic eye.

Maybe it's a fossil—
some rare combination
of obsidian & onyx fused together,
excavated from a seam of coal
& conjured into day.

Or the words that drift
in & out of a swing-low dream
in the middle of the night.

What you find on a porch
between friends in summer
amid the moths & moonlight.

The bittersweet dredge
of a charred oak barrel
welded into spirits

& sipped ceremoniously
from a wide-mouthed jar.

Maybe it's what happens
when a cacophony of tongues rise
against so, so many bullets
destined for Black skin.

Or that you won't recognize it
until it shows up unbidden,
a howling maelstrom on your
doorstep that you dare not turn away.

Maybe it's all of these.

Whatever it is,
it's a mystery—
you won't ever know
until you break down & grow
your own.

RANE ARROYO was a poet, playwright, and professor. He received his PhD in English and Cultural Studies from the University of Pittsburgh, and taught at the University of Toledo until his unexpected death in 2010. His poetry collections include, *The Singing Shark, Home Movies of Narcissus, The Portable Famine, Same-Sex Seances, The Buried Sea: New & Selected Poems*, and *The Sky's Weight*. He also published a book of stories, *How to Name a Hurricane*, and several plays.

A. H. JERRIOD AVANT is from Longtown, MS. A graduate of Jackson State University, he's earned MFA degrees from Spalding University and New York University. An Affrilachian Poet and graduate of the Callaloo Creative Writing Workshop, his poems have appeared in the *Mississippi Review, Boston Review, pluck!, Pinwheel* and *Callaloo*. A finalist for the 2015 Mississippi Review Prize, Jerriod is the 2016–2017, 2nd-year Poetry Fellow at the Fine Arts Work Center in Provincetown.

MAKALANI BANDELE has received fellowships from the Kentucky Arts Council, Cave Canem, and Millay Colony. He is member of the Affrilachian Poets. His work has been published in several anthologies, and in many in print and online in literary magazines. He is the author of one book of poems, *hellfightin'* (Willow Books, 2012).

REMICA BINGHAM-RISHER earned an MFA from Bennington College, is a Cave Canem fellow and a member of the Affrilachian Poets. Her first book, *Conversion* (Lotus, 2006), won the Naomi Long Madgett Poetry Award. Her second book, *What We Ask of Flesh* (Etruscan, 2013), was shortlisted for the Hurston/Wright Legacy Award. Her third book, *Starlight & Error* (Diode, 2017), won the Diode Editions Book Award.

BERNARD CLAY is a Kentucky native raised mostly in Louisville. He currently lives in Frankfort with his wife and dog where he is pursuing a MFA in poetry from the University of Kentucky. He is a member of the Affrilachian Poets and his work has appeared in journals and other publications.

GERALD L. COLEMAN, cofounder of the Affrilachian Poets, studied Philosophy, English, and Religious Studies, culminating in a MA in Theology. Author of the fantasy novel, *When Night Falls: Book One of The Three Gifts*, and poetry collections, *the road is long* and *falling to earth*, you can find him at geraldlcoleman.co.

MITCHELL L. H. DOUGLAS, Associate Professor of English at Indiana University-Purdue University Indianapolis (IUPUI), is a founding member of the Affrilachian Poets, a Cave Canem Fellow, and poetry editor for *pluck! The Journal of Affrilachian Arts & Culture*. His second poetry collection *blak\ \al-fə bet*, winner of the 2011 Lexi Rudnitsky/Editor's Choice Award, is available from Persea Books. His debut collection, *Cooling Board: A Long-Playing Poem*, was a runner-up for the 2007 Stan and Tom Wick Poetry Prize, a semifinalist for the 2007 Blue Lynx Prize, and a semifinalist for the 2006 Crab Orchard Series in Poetry First Book Award. In 2010, *Cooling Board* was nominated for an NAACP Image Award in the Outstanding Literary Work-Poetry category and a Hurston/Wright Legacy Award.

KELLY NORMAN ELLIS, author of *Tougaloo Blues* (2003) and *Offerings of Desire* (2012). Her poetry has appeared in *Sisterfire: Black Womanist Fiction and Poetry, Spirit and Flame, Role Call: A Generational Anthology of Social and Political Black Literature and Art, Boomer Girls, Essence Magazine, Obsidian, Calyx,* and *Cornbread Nation.* She is a recipient of a Kentucky Foundation for Women writer's grant and is a Cave Canem fellow and founding member of the Affrilachian Poets. Ellis is an associate professor of English and creative writing and chairperson for the Department of English, Foreign Languages and Literatures at Chicago State University.

NIKKY FINNEY was born in South Carolina, within listening distance of the sea. A child of activists, she came of age during the civil rights and Black Arts Movements. At Talladega College, nurtured by Hale Woodruff's Amistad murals, Finney began to understand the powerful synergy between art and history. Finney has authored four books of poetry: *Head Off & Split* (2011); *The World Is Round* (2003); *Rice* (1995); and *On Wings Made of Gauze* (1985). The John H. Bennett, Jr. Chair in Creative Writing and Southern Letters at the University of South Carolina, Finney also authored *Heartwood* (1997), edited *The Ringing Ear: Black Poets Lean South* (2007), and co-founded the Affrilachian Poets. Finney's fourth book of poetry, *Head Off & Split,* was awarded the 2011 National Book Award for poetry.

ASHA FRENCH is a poet and essayist. She writes about parenting her favorite daughter, mourning her favorite father, and learning how to love women in ways that heal. She has a spirit guide in the person of a five year old daughter who loves bats. Her work has appeared in *pluck!, PoetryMemoirStory, Emory Magazine, Mutha Magazine, Women's Media Project,* and *Autostraddle.* She is a former columnist for Ebony.com and is currently looking for a home for her collection of essays.

CRYSTAL DAWN GOOD was born on a clear morning. She is a Writer Poet. Quantum Christian. Tunk Player. Libra Charmer. Underdog Cheerleader. Dethroned Affrilachian Homecoming Queen. Occasionally she performs with Heroes Are Gang Leaders, a New York-based Free/Avant-Garde experimental improvisation ensemble. She was elected in 2014 to the made-up-but-completely-real office of Social Media Senator for the Digital District of West Virginia. "Senator Good" uses poetry and performance to explore the landscape of West Virginia aka The Heart of Appalachia as a lens into the meta-universe. Crystal is the author of *Valley Girl.*

ELLEN HAGAN is a writer, performer, and educator. Her latest collection of poetry *Hemisphere,* was published by Northwestern University Press, Spring 2015. Her first collection of poetry, *Crowned* was published by Sawyer House Press in 2010. Ellen recently joined the poetry faculty at West Virginia Wesleyan in their low-residency MFA program. She is the Director of Poetry and Theatre Programs at the DreamYard Project in the Bronx and directs their International Poetry Exchange with school partners in Japan and South Korea. She lives with her husband and daughters in New York City.

DORIAN HAIRSTON is a poet, scholar, and former college athlete from Lexington, KY. He is an Affrilachian Poet and his work has appeared in *pluck!*, *Anthology of Appalachian Writers*, and *Shale*. He currently lives in Lexington where he is completing his MFA in Creative Writing at the University of Kentucky.

RANDALL HORTON is the author of three collections of poetry and most recently, *Hook: A Memoir* (Augury Books 2015). He is an Affrilachian Poet, a member of the experimental performance group, 'Heroes Are Gang Leaders,' and Associate Professor of English at the University of New Haven.

AMANDA JOHNSTON earned a Master of Fine Arts in Creative Writing from the University of Southern Maine. Her poetry and interviews have appeared in numerous online and print publications, among them, *Kinfolks Quarterly*, *Muzzle*, *pluck!* and the anthologies, *Small Batch*, *di-ver-city* and *The Ringing Ear: Black Poets Lean South*. The recipient of multiple Artist Enrichment grants from the Kentucky Foundation for Women and the Christina Sergeyevna Award from the Austin International Poetry Festival, she is a member of the Affrilachian Poets and a Cave Canem graduate fellow. Johnston is a Stonecoast MFA faculty member, a co-founder of Black Poets Speak Out, and founding executive director of Torch Literary Arts.

NORMAN JORDAN, a native of Ansted, West Virginia, co-founded the African-American Heritage Family Tree Museum and the African American Arts and Heritage Academy. His poetry has been anthologized in many books, including, *Make a Joyful Sound: Poems for Children by African-American Poets*, *In Search of Color Everywhere: A Collection of African-American Poetry* and *Wild Sweet Notes: Fifty Years of West Virginia Poetry*.

SHAYLA LAWSON is (and / or, at times, has been) an amateur acrobat, an architect, a Dutch housewife, & dog mother to one irascible hound. Her work has appeared in print and online at ESPN, *The Offing*, *Guernica*, *Colorado Review*, *Barrelhouse*, *The Journal*, *South Dakota Review*, *Winter Tangerine Review*, *111O*, *inter|rupture*, *pluck!*, *Indiana Review*, & *MiPOesias* (among others). She is the former Nonfiction Editor of Indiana Review, the inaugural winner of Sou'Wester's Robbins Award in Poetry, honorably mentioned in the back of the 2016 Pushcart Anthology, & author of three poetry collections: *A Speed Education in Human Being*, *PANTONE*, & the forthcoming *I Think I'm Ready to See Frank Ocean*. Her work has been supported by fellowships provided through Callaloo, the Kentucky Foundation for Women, the Giorgio Cini Foundation of Venice, Italy, & The Peggy Guggenheim Collection.

Raised somewhere between the tobacco fields and horse farms of Woodford County, Kentucky, **JUDE McPHERSON** has been bending and stretching syllables as long as he can remember. A member of the Affrilachian Poets, his first full length collection of poetry 'on my mind' is a reflection of his eclectic personality. He has published two previous collections of poetry through blacoetry press; *loves taxicab blues revisited* (1998) and t*he book of jude* (2000).

MARTA MARIA MIRANDA-STRAUB is Afro-Caribbean and identifies as "Cubalachian": Cuban by birth and Appalachian by the Grace of God. She has a forty year career as a social worker, educator, scholar, administrator, activist and community organizer. Her life focus has been the promotion of equity and social justice. She writes about issues of identity and place, she is a published author, poet and story-teller, Marta was inducted into the Affrilachian Poets in 2006. She is currently working on her memoir, *Cradled by Skeletons: A Life in Poems.*

KAMILAH AISHA MOON is a recipient of fellowships to the Cave Canem Foundation, the Prague Summer Writing Institute, the Fine Arts Work Center in Provincetown, MA, and the Vermont Studio Center, Moon's work has been featured in several journals and anthologies, including *Harvard Review, jubilat, Poem-A-Day* for the Academy of American Poets, *Oxford American, Lumina, Callaloo, Essence, Gathering Ground.* A Pushcart Prize winner, she was also a finalist for the Lambda Literary Award and the Audre Lorde Award from the Publishing Triangle. She has taught English and Creative Writing for several colleges and organizations. Moon holds an MFA in Creative Writing from Sarah Lawrence College. A native of Nashville, TN, she currently lives in Brooklyn, NY.

A poet and scholar, **SHAUNA M. MORGAN, PH.D.** is the author of *Fear of Dogs & Other Animals* and she teaches literature of the African Diaspora at Howard University in Washington, D.C. Her current research focuses on representations of Black womanhood and Neo-anticolonialism in 21st century literature. Her poems have appeared in *ProudFlesh: New Afrikan Journal of Culture, Politics & Consciousness, Anthology of Appalachian Writers Volume VI, Interviewing the Caribbean*, and elsewhere. Her critical work can be found in the *Bulletin of the School of Oriental and African Studies, Journal of Postcolonial Writing*, and *South Atlantic Review.*

RICARDO NAZARIO Y COLÓN is the author of *The Recital* from Winged City Chapbooks 2011 and *Of Jibaros and Hillbillies* from Plain View Press 2011. Visit him at http://www.lalomadelviento.com.

JEREMY PADEN is an Associate Professor of Spanish at Transylvania University in Lexington, KY. and he teaches literary translation in Spalding University's low-residency MFA. He received his PhD in Colonial Latin American literature from Emory University. He is the author of two chapbooks of poems: *Broken Tulips* (Accents Publishing, 2013) and *ruina montium* (Broadstone Press, 2016). He is also the author a chapbook of translated poems: *Delicate Matters* (Winged City Chapbooks, 2016).

JOY PRIEST is a writer from Louisville, Kentucky. She is the winner of the 2016 Hurston/Wright Foundation's College Writers Award, and a 2015 Kentucky Arts Council Emerging Artist Award. Joy has received grants, scholarships, and fellowships from the Fine Arts Work Center, the Bread Loaf Writers' Conference, and the University of South Carolina where she is a writing instructor and MFA candidate in poetry. Her work has appeared or is upcoming in *Best New Poets 2014 & 2016, The BreakBeat Poets, Blackbird, Callaloo, Drunken Boat*, and *Muzzle*, among others.

STEPHANIE PRUITT is a poet and social practice artist who has taught at Vanderbilt University, the Sewanee Young Writers' Conference, and as a visiting artist in over one hundred K-12 and community settings. She is the recipient of an Academy of American Poets Prize and Essence Magazine named her one of their "40 Favorite Poets." Stephanie serves as a Commissioner for Metro Arts and on the board of directors for the Arts & Business Council. She prefers flip flops over stilettos, pancakes over waffles, and the toilet paper is always over, not under. When at her Nashville home, the mother of Nia and wife of Al can often be found with an 70lb dog in her lap. The TEDx speaker is the founder of NoStarvingArtist(dot)me and is committed to helping creators make a LIFE and LIVING with their art.

DANNI QUINTOS is a knitter and a Kentuckian. She received her MFA in Poetry from Indiana University, where she taught Creative Writing and served as an Associate Poetry Editor for Indiana Review. Her work has appeared or is forthcoming in *Day One*, *pluck!*, *Anthropoid*, *Rabbit Catastrophe Review*, *Best New Poets 2015* and elsewhere. She lives in Lexington with her husband Zach and their Ren & Stimpy cat-dog duo. Rumor has it, she is knitting a cocoon, from which she will emerge when her first book manuscript is finished.

SHANNA L. SMITH is a Visiting Assistant Professor in the Department of English and Modern Foreign Languages at Jackson State University. She earned her doctorate in American Studies, specializing in African American Literature and Culture, at the University of Maryland College Park. A native of Kentucky, Smith is an Affrilachian Poet.

BIANCA LYNNE SPRIGGS is an award-winning writer and multidisciplinary artist from Lexington, Kentucky. The author of four collections of poetry, her most recent are *Call Her By Her Name* (Northwestern University Press, 2016) and *The Galaxy Is a Dance Floor* (Argos Books, 2016). She is the managing editor for *pluck! The Journal of Affrilachian Arts & Culture* and the poetry editor for *Apex Magazine*. You can learn more about her work at: www.biancaspriggs.com

PAUL C. TAYLOR teaches philosophy and African American Studies at Pennsylvania State University. His scholarly books include *On Obama and Black is Beautiful: A Philosophy of Black Aesthetics*. He is also an Affrilachian Poet, with short stories and poetry in *Limestone, The Harvard Advocate*, and elsewhere.

Multidisciplinary artist and Danville, Kentucky native, FRANK X WALKER, is the former Poet Laureate of Kentucky and Professor in the department of English and African American and Africana Studies Program at the University of Kentucky. The founding editor of *pluck!* is a Cave Canem fellow, co-founder of the Affrilachian Poets, and the author of eight collections of poetry.

CRYSTAL WILKINSON is the author of *Blackberries, Blackberries*, winner of the 2002 Chaffin Award for Appalachian Literature and *Water Street*, a finalist for both the UK's Orange Prize for Fiction and the Hurston/Wright Legacy Award. Both books are published by Toby Press . She is also the recipient of awards and fellowships from The Kentucky Foundation for Women, The Kentucky Arts Council, The Mary

Anderson Center for the Arts and the Archie D. and Bertha H. Walker Scholarship Fund at the Fine Arts Work Center in Provincetown. She currently teaches at Berea College. Her novel, *The Birds of Opulence*, was the 2016 recipient of the Ernest J. Gaines Award for Literary Excellence. She and her partner, artist Ron Davis, are the owners of an independent bookstore, The Wild Fig.

KEITH S. WILSON is an Affrilachian Poet, Cave Canem fellow, and graduate of the Callaloo Creative Writing Workshop. He has received three scholarships from Bread Loaf and scholarships from the Millay Colony, MacDowell, and Ucross. Keith serves as assistant poetry editor at *Four Way Review* and digital media editor at *Obsidian Journal*.

Born in Banner Elk, NC, **FORREST GRAY YERMAN** is an independent scholar whose work focuses on the Affrilachian Poets. He holds an MA in Appalachian Studies and a BA in Creative Writing, both from Appalachian State University. He has published in *Appalachian Journal, Valley Voices*, and the *Mildred Haun Review*.

Root

Paul C. Taylor
> "Call Me Out My Name"; (*pluck! The Journal of Affrilachian Arts & Culture* 2011)

Frank X Walker
> "Affrilachia" (*Affrilachia*, Old Cove Press 2000)

Nikky Finney
> "Brown Country" (*Rice: Poems.* Copyright © 2013 by Nikky Finney. First edition copyright © 1995 by Lynn Carol Nikky Finney. First published in Toronto [Ontario, Canada] in paperback in 1995 by Sister Vision: Black Women and Women of Colour Press. Published in 2013 by TriQuarterly Books/Northwestern University Press by arrangement with Nikky Finney. All rights reserved.)

Ricardo Nazario y Colón
> "Tujcalusa" (Of *Jibaros and Hillbillies*; Plain View Press 2010)

Ellen Hagan
> "Grits" (*Duende Magazine*; October 2014)

Joy Priest
> "In the City" (*Toe Good Poetry* 2014)

Makalani Bandele
> "fleur-de-lis" (*The Louisville Review*; Special Kentucky Issue 2012)
> "On Aging" (*Small Batch: an anthology of bourbon poetry*; two of cups press 2013)

Bianca Lynne Spriggs
> "Praisesong for a Mountain" (*The Chattahoochee Review*, 2016; The Galaxy Is a Dance Floor 2016)

Jeremy Paden
> "The Hills We Grew On" (*Duende Magazine*; October 2014)

Limb

Ricardo Nazario y Colón
> "Of Jíbaros and Hillbillies" (*Of Jíbaros and Hillbillies*; Plain View Press 2010)

Kelly Norman Ellis
"Raised by Women" (Coal Black Voices 2001)

Remica Bingham-Risher
"Portrait of Mother's Kitchen" (*Conversion*, Lotus Press 2007)

Frank X Walker
"Burying Albatross" (*Affrilachian Sonnets*, Larkspur 2016)

Rane Arroyo
"Even Tricksters Get the Blues" (*White as Silver*, Cervená Barva Press 2010)

Shayla Lawson
"Pantone 130C" (*Pantone*, miel 2016)

Danni Quintos
"Pond's White Beauty" (*Best New Poets* 2015)
"Portrait of My Dad Through a Tent Window" (*Rabbit Catastrophe Review* 2017)

Joy Priest
"Nightstick" (*Best New Poets* 2014)

Keith S. Wilson
"Robatto Mulatto" (Anti-, 2010)

Tongue

Kamilah Aisha Moon
"Initiation" (*The Offing* 2015)

Rane Arroyo
"The Piñata Boy" (*Same Sex-Seances*, New Sins Press 2008)

Norman Jordan
"One eyed critics" (*Where Do People in Dreams Come From?*, Museum Press 2014)
"Where Do People in Dreams Come From?" (*Where Do People in Dreams Come From?*, Museum Press 2014)